D1455454

DEVELOPING MANAGERS AS COACHES

Latest titles in the McGraw-Hill Training Series

DELIVERING 'IN-HOUSE' OUTPLACEMENT
A Practical Guide for Trainers, Managers and Personnel Specialists
Alan Jones   ISBN 0-07-707895-0

FACILITATION
Providing Opportunities For Learning
Trevor Bentley   ISBN 0-07-707684-2

DEVELOPMENT CENTRES
Realizing the Potential of Your Employees Through Assessment and Development
Geoff Lee and David Beard   ISBN 0-07-707785-7

DEVELOPING DIRECTORS
Building An Effective Boardroom Team
Colin Coulson-Thomas   ISBN 0-07-707590-0

MANAGING THE TRAINING PROCESS
Putting the Basics into Practice
Mike Wills   ISBN 0-07-707806-3

RESOURCE-BASED LEARNING
Using Open and Flexible Resources for Continuous Development
Julie Dorrell   ISBN 0-07-707692-3

WORKSHOPS THAT WORK
100 Ideas to Make Your Training Events More Effective
Tom Bourner, Vivien Martin, Phil Race   ISBN 0-07-707800-4

THE HANDBOOK FOR ORGANIZATIONAL CHANGE
Strategy and Skill for Trainers and Developers
Carol A. O'Connor   ISBN 0-07-707693-1

TRAINING FOR PROFIT
A Guide to the Integration of Training in an Organization's Success
Philip Darling   ISBN 0-07-707786-5

TEAM BUILDING
A Practical Guide for Trainers
Neil Clark   ISBN 0-07-707846-2

DEVELOPING MANAGERS AS COACHES
A Trainer's Guide
Frank Salisbury   ISBN 0-07-707892-6

THE ASSERTIVE TRAINER
A Practical Guide for Trainers
Liz Willis and Jenny Daisley   ISBN 0-07-707077-2

LEARNING TO CHANGE
A Resource for Trainers, Managers and Learners Based on Self-organized Learning
Sheila Harri-Augstein and Ian M. Webb   ISBN 0-07-707896-9

ASSESSMENT AND DEVELOPMENT IN EUROPE
Adding value to individuals and organizations
Marc Bolton   ISBN 0-07-707928-0

Details of these and other titles in the series are available from:

The Product Manager, Professional Books, McGraw-Hill Book Company Europe,
Shoppenhangers Road, Maidenhead, Berkshire SL6 2QL, United Kingdom
Tel: 01628 23432 Fax: 01628 770224

Developing managers as coaches

A trainer's guide

Frank S. Salisbury

McGRAW-HILL BOOK COMPANY

London · New York · St Louis · San Francisco · Auckland
Bogotá · Caracas · Lisbon · Madrid · Mexico · Milan
Montreal · New Delhi · Panama · Paris · San Juan · São Paulo
Singapore · Sydney · Tokyo · Toronto

Published by
McGRAW-HILL Book Company Europe
Shoppenhangers Road, Maidenhead, Berkshire, SL6 2QL, England
Telephone: 01628 23432
Fax: 01628 770224

British Library Cataloguing in Publication Data
Salisbury, Frank S.
    Developing Managers as Coaches: Trainer's
    Guide. – (McGraw-Hill Training Series)
    I. Title   II. Series
    658.3

    ISBN 0-07-707892-6

Library of Congress Cataloging-in-Publication Data
Salisbury, Frank S.,
    Developing managers as coaches: a trainer's guide/Frank S.
Salisbury
        p.   cm. – (McGraw-Hill training series)
    Includes bibliographical references and index.
    ISBN 0-07-707892-6
    1. Executive ability.   2. Mentors in business.   3. Executives–
Training of.   I. Title.   II. Series.
    HD38.2.S25   1994   94-5771
    658.4'07124–dc20   CIP

McGraw-Hill
A Division of *The McGraw·Hill Companies*

Copyright © 1994 McGraw-Hill International (UK) Limited. All rights reserved.
No part of this publication may be reproduced, stored in a retrieval system, or
transmitted, in any form or by any means, electronic, mechanical, photocopying,
recording, or otherwise, without the prior permission of McGraw-Hill International
(UK) Limited.

45 CUP 976

Typeset by BookEns Limited, Royston, Herts.
and printed and bound in Great Britain
at the University Press, Cambridge

Printed on permanent paper in compliance with ISO Standard 9706

For Pauline, Michael and Helen

Contents

Series preface

Training and development are now firmly centre stage in most organizations, if not all. Nothing unusual in that—for some organizations. They have always seen training and development as part of the heart of their businesses—but more and more must see it that same way.

The demographic trends through the 1990s will inject into the marketplace severe competition for good people who will need good training. Young people without conventional qualifications, skilled workers in redundant crafts, people out of work, women wishing to return to work—all will require excellent training to fit them to meet the job demands of the 1990s and beyond.

But excellent training does not spring from what we have done well in the past. T&D specialists are in a new ball game. 'Maintenance' training—training to keep up skill levels to do what we have always done—will be less in demand. Rather, organization, work and market change training are now much more important and will remain so for some time. Changing organizations and people is no easy task, requiring special skills and expertise which, sadly, many T&D specialists do not possess.

To work as a 'change' specialist requires us to get to centre stage—to the heart of the company's business. This means we have to ask about future goals and strategies, and even be involved in their development, at least as far as T&D policies are concerned.

This demands excellent communication skills, political expertise, negotiating ability, diagnostic skills—indeed, all the skills a good internal consultant requires.

The implications for T&D specialists are considerable. It is not enough merely to be skilled in the basics of training, we must also begin to act like business people and to think in business terms and talk the language of business. We must be able to resource training not just from within but by using the vast array of external resources. We must be able to manage our activities as well as any other manager. We must share in the creation and communication of the company's vision. We must never let the goals of the company out of our sight.

In short, we may have to grow and change with the business. It will be hard. We shall not only have to demonstrate relevance but also value for money and achievement of results. We shall be our own boss, as accountable for results as any other line manager, and we shall have to deal with fewer internal resources.

The challenge is on, as many T&D specialists have demonstrated to me over the past few years. We need to be capable of meeting that challenge. This is why McGraw-Hill Book Company Europe have planned and launched this major new training series—to help us meet that challenge.

The series covers all aspects of T&D and provides the knowledge base from which we can develop plans to meet the challenge. They are practical books for the professional person. They are a starting point for planning our journey into the twenty-first century.

Use them well. Don't just read them. Highlight key ideas, thoughts, action pointers or whatever, and have a go at doing something with them. Through experimentation we evolve; through stagnation we die.

I know that all the authors in the McGraw-Hill Training Series would want me to wish you good luck. Have a great journey into the twenty-first century.

ROGER BENNETT
Series Editor

About the series editor

Roger Bennett has over 20 years' experience in training, management education, research and consulting. He has long been involved with trainer training and trainer effectiveness. He has carried out research into trainer effectiveness, and conducted workshops, seminars, and conferences on the subject around the world. He has written extensively on the subject including the book *Improving Trainer Effectiveness*, Gower. His work has taken him all over the world and has involved directors of companies as well as managers and trainers.

Dr Bennett has worked in engineering, several business schools (including the International Management Centre, where he launched the UK's first master's degree in T&D), and has been a board director of two companies. He is the editor of the *Journal of European Industrial Training* and was series editor of the ITD's *Get In There* workbook and video package for the managers of training departments. He now runs his own business called The Management Development Consultancy.

Preface

The seeds of greatness

With ten of my colleagues I had just scaled a wall which stretched endlessly skyward, or was it really only 4 metres high? Scaling implies some kind of professional approach, when in fact, most of us, men and women, had been hauled over it, quite unceremoniously. It was at the end of a long two days, where we had climbed mountains, crossed ravines, walked along dangerous obstacles, and with careless abandon thrown ourselves from great heights into the waiting arms of companions. Our journey was along the 'Challenge of Excellence' during which our course tutors David Hemery and Susan Kaye had sparked our imagination, stimulated our desire to succeed, and watered the seeds of our greatness.

It was David who first told me about the seed of greatness. He believes that each and every one of us has that seed within us. On completing the Challenge of Excellence, while my sense of achievement knew no bounds, I was unsure about the greatness of the seed. In hindsight he was right. We all have it.

For me it was one of the major milestones in a long project to discover a better way of managing and of training and developing people. I had been working for nearly two years previously, convinced that coaching from the athletic world could be combined with managerial motivational psychology, to form a more effective style of developing and managing others than was currently being practised in most companies.

My field of expertise has been in the field of sales training, and for most of the time in this area I believed that to be an effective sales trainer, you had to have had a track record as a successful salesperson. That narrow, but seemingly plausible belief has often been mirrored by colleagues and acquaintances from other disciplines. Try and find a teacher who supports business managers becoming headteachers. What difficulties have the externally appointed National Health Service executives faced in settling into their new roles? It is not only actors who get typecast in a role, so do managers, salespeople, and every other professional who changes from practitioner to trainer. Few people argue with the point of view that to be a good trainer, you must have a good track record performing the function you are training others in—few, that is, except those doing it. Some might argue that it is pointless the blind leading the blind, and I have to say that all too often I have seen trainers trying to deliver something from a textbook or course manual, unable to deviate from the timetable for fear of being caught out.

While it is true to say that I have met a large number of mediocre trainers lacking the requisite job knowledge and application, the experience of working on the coaching model shown in this book has thrown some of that theory into doubt. I have coached people to sell products I know nothing about. I have coached people to play better snooker and golf, when my own skills in both leave a lot to be desired. I have observed coaches improving the skills of managers, without themselves having been in management. Granted, coaches need a knowledge of the job to be done, but they need to be neither proficient nor expert in the role being coached.

What is required, though, is that the person being coached has a basic knowledge or understanding of the skill being coached before coaching can be successfully achieved by someone not personally accomplished or knowledgeable in the skill.

People have to be trained to do the basic job, after which time they can be coached to improve. Those operating as trainers, in most cases, need to have first-hand experience of the job; those coaching, require different attributes and skills.

As coaches it is also essential to have complete belief in the potential of individuals. Each of us can ultimately do anything we want to, given sufficient time, opportunity and motivation. We only use a fraction of the skills we are born with to achieve, in the same way that we utilize a mere fragment of the potential of our brains. I assert that there is the seed of greatness in us all, but like most of us I had to have the 'Doubting Thomas' side of my nature pandered to in order truly to believe it, and act upon it.

Throughout my previous research (M.Phil. 1985), into the effectiveness of training, the influence of the manager became a recurring theme. I am convinced that training fails to deliver primarily due to line management's apathy and the lack of support for field training activity. However, line management is not solely responsible for this situation. The problem is exacerbated by the trainer's inability to show the manager any real lasting benefit from training. Trainers and managers are as far apart from each other these days as they have ever been—each one blaming the other for performance shortfalls in trainees. Two common enough statements from both camps that are heard are:

MANAGERS   If those people in training only came down from their theoretical towers and tried dealing with reality it might do them the world of good.

TRAINERS   What's the point of training people simply to send them into the clutches of a management team oblivious to the needs of continuous training?

Neither statement is helpful—to the relationship between trainers and managers, or to the organization and the rest of the people working in it.

What coaching has done for me, and it can do the same for you, is to bring managers and trainers together, focusing on a common goal, using the same ball, and playing as a team on a level playing field. By the use of a common philosophy and language, I have observed a change in the manager/trainer relationship which produces in each a trust of the skills possessed by each player, and the desire of each to excel and to have their charges excel. The premiss is that each person can excel at a job, given the opportunity and assistance to do so.

In terms of the skills we have and can acquire, at the moment of birth we are all equal. We have the genes of our parents, but external factors being equal, we all have the same opportunity for greatness. I know that those external factors soon play a major role in influencing our journey and eventual destination. I know that there are limiting factors based upon birthright and that some things are not possible. I accept that my children cannot rise to the first office of the United States. I concede, reluctantly, that my son can never become king. It is plainly evident that I will not now score the winning goal for Newcastle United in a FA Cup Final (whether that has to do with my ability or physique is debatable. No, it is definitely to do with my physique!)

These and other similar self-evident truths aside, I firmly profess that managers, computer programmers, doctors, lawyers, clerks, drivers, salespeople, and 1000 other job holders, whether classified as professionals or not, are not born to that profession but are fabricated into it by their environment and chance. Correspondingly, road sweepers, ditch diggers, the unemployed and the unemployable, are not a product of genetic certainty, but of circumstance, opportunity, and most importantly the loving care and attention of their seed of greatness, or perhaps even the lack of it.

All employees have it within themselves to deliver a personal performance of excellence outside of their currently perceived limit of aspiration. My contention is, supported by my own experience and practical research into management, that people at work have greater aspirations than either the manager realizes, or that they share with their manager. The difference between those who deliver and those who do not, is undoubtedly the manager, together with the individual's acceptance of personal responsibility, and the manager's acceptance of his or her own overall accountability. I propose that the manager who operates as a coach can bring the seed of greatness to the surface in all its glory. I advance the suggestion that managers who rid themselves of the normal managerial traits of controlling, delegating, decision making, and most importantly telling, and adopt the principles espoused in this book will reap the harvest of the seeds of greatness within their staff.

The greatest problem for managers and trainers, however, is to give up telling other people what to do, when it is appropriate. Managers, and trainers seem not to understand this. Phrases like 'She's a natural leader', 'He takes charge immediately', 'They lead from the front. They tell you what's what, and how it's going to be done', and similar, advocate that leading and managing is about telling people what to do. It is a natural enough phenomenon. We grow up being told what to do by our parents, it is something we expect, and usually receive. It is hardly surprising, therefore, that when we as parents are presented with our own off-spring we fall into the telling trap. Many may argue that this is necessary. What is certainly not necessary and less desirable is that when we become trainers, and managers ourselves, we tend constantly to tell others what to do. Certainly there are occasions when telling is required. Coaching someone through an emergency may result in empowerment of the individual, but also injury.

The educational system from primary to secondary school continues the processes of telling, and for the vast majority of people entry into the labour system exposes us to yet further instructions. Those leaving secondary school and entering the more liberal environment of colleges and universities represent a small and lamentably declining minority in terms of a percentage of the total population. It is not the shortage of continuing education that I perceive harms the seed of greatness, it is the lack of confidence that an early entry into a poorly managed labour system brings about. This lack of education of the early workforce is reinforced by the majority of managers who receive no formal training or education themselves either upon or following appointment.

Many managers confuse coaching with being soft, showing weakness when what is required is strength. Coaching is not a soft option. It requires strength of character. It requires managers to be strong in their belief that employees have the solution to their performance problems within them. It requires managers to have the courage to let go.

Coaching is also confused with counselling. It can be similar, but it is not the same. The British Association for Counselling (BAC) defines counselling as:

the skilled and principal use of relationship to facilitate self-knowledge, emotional acceptance and growth, and the optimal development of personal resources.

In coaching, as in counselling, the answer to performance problems and potential lies within each individual, and as with the counsellor, those answers can be extracted by careful and systematic questioning. To that end, coaching also seeks to bring about a self-awareness in those being coached. In coaching roles within organizations however, the coach has a clear objective to focus people on performance issues. The coach has a goal, and that goal is almost always tied in with organizational objectives. Managers as coaches also have an additional responsibility and accountability and are, therefore, additionally concerned with time-scales. The seed of greatness has to be tended and nurtured, but it also has to provide and to deliver. Coaches are not counsellors. Many managers believe that coaching and counselling are the same and dismiss coaching as a weak alternative to instructing. As a coach you have a responsibility to move people forward towards a corporate aim. That movement forward involves expense, and therefore the company coach is acutely aware of when to pull the plug. As a counsellor, you do not have that responsibility. You may have the desire to move people forward, but the responsibility for the time-scale rests with the individual.

This book is about a new way of developing, managing and empowering people. This book is about adopting coaching as a concept, a practice and a process. The concept is contained within the book if you look for it. It should be embodied within your own beliefs about people and about their untapped abilities. The concept holds that most people want to contribute more than they currently are allowed to; that people want to belong and to be in control of their own destinies, but that somewhere along the journey they were hijacked. The practice requires a transference from the theory of the classroom to the reality of work. It requires managers to release people from the chains of telling and of rules and regulations and conformity. It requires managers to understand that subordinates have the same feelings of responsibility as they do, and that trust is something to be shared—it is a two way process. But trusting is a risky business—'I tried that once and it didn't work!' So try it again until it does. The process is in the use of the POWER model.

The book is for trainers of managers, and for managers being trained. Whether as coach, or as someone being coached, there should be something here for you. Anyone can be a coach, in any situation, providing there exists a genuine desire for these coaching principles. There also needs to be a shared vision, trust and mutual support. Furthermore, coaches need to believe in the premiss that all people can grow. Coaches must have a clear vision of that growth, both for themselves and for the people with whom they work. The greatest gift a coach can give is time—time to coach.

This book focuses on the coaching model 'POWER' which stands for *P*urpose, *O*bjectives, *W*hat is happening now?, *E*mpowering and *R*eview. Using the techniques suggested, trainers and managers will be able to increase the successes they have with their trainees. I use the word trainee in the widest sense, encompassing anyone who is in learning mode. I am a trainee, and hopefully will remain so. To stop learning is to stop living. The most important thing we can do as trainers is to encourage others to keep learning. To do that trainers, managers and coaches have to lead by example. The worst anyone can do is to assume that he or she has heard it all before—'Been there, seen that, got the T-shirt'—and the commonest barrier to increased ability is usually the existence of restricted vision and a closed mind. Coaching is not another one-year-only panacea. It is an integral part of a whole development programme, but for a change, one which works.

A major problem with many development programmes is that they constantly shift direction depending upon the whims of the incumbent training manager or chief executive. If you want coaching to work, as it can, then you will also have to decide that you will stick with it until you and your managers get it right, and that could take as long as it takes. Some multinational organizations have a five-year plan; a few have a ten-year plan. For anything to embed itself properly, it takes that length of time. It also displays to the troops your commitment to making something work. That philosophy unfortunately does not fit in with Western business culture. We tend to work to smaller time-scales. I know of some companies who cannot see further than the quarter-end figures, and then they wonder why no planning takes place. The Japanese have a greater vision of the future, with many of their companies operating a 20-year planning policy. One Japanese firm is purported to have a 250-year plan! Whichever way you approach it, everybody in the company needs to understand the longevity of your coaching plans and philosophy.

The seed of greatness exists for all those who say they *can*, and even within those who say they *cannot*. Coaching can release that seed, not just for the person being coached, but also for the coach. This book could change your performance for the better. It has represented for me a model upon which personal performance issues are clearly defined, structured and acted upon; it could do the same for you, and for the people you seek to develop. It is the missing piece of the development jigsaw.

Recommended reading

Albrecht, Karl (1980) *Brain Power*. Prentice-Hall, NJ.

Bristol, Claude M. (1985) *The Magic of Believing*. Prentice-Hall, NJ.

Burdett, John O. (1991) 'To coach, or not to coach—that is the question!', *Industrial and Commercial Training*, **23**(5).

Buzan, Tony (1974) *Use Your Head*. BBC Books.

Clarkson, Petruska (1991) 'Counselling, psychotherapy, psychology and psychiatry', *Employee Counselling Today*, **3**(3).

Dick, Frank (1991) 'Fitness to win', *Target—Management Development Review*. **4**(3), MCB University Press.

Forster, Steve (1991) 'Hemery's Way', *Management Week*, 18 September.

Gallwey, W. Timothy (1974) *The Inner Game of Tennis*. Pan.

Hemery MBE, David (1991) *Sporting Excellence: What Makes a Champion?* Collins Willow.

Hemery MBE, David (1991) 'Sports star lessons for managers', *Target—Management Development Review*, **4**(3), MCB University Press.

James, Muriel and Jongeward, Dorothy (1971) *Born to Win*. Addison-Wesley Inc.

Maltz, Maxwell and Powers, Melvin (1960) *Psycho-cybernetics*. Prentice-Hall, NJ.

Patmore, Bob (1991) *Bob Patmore's Perfect Vision*. Granta Editions.

Robbins, Anthony (1988) *Unlimited Power*. Simon and Schuster.

Royce, William S. (1988) 'How to be a business coach', *Journal of Management Consulting*, **4**(2).

Whitmore, John (1992) *Coaching for Performance*. Nicholas Brearley Publishing.

Acknowledgements

It took quite some time to research and write this book and there are some people who deserve mention for the help and inspiration they gave me. They have in one way or another helped me to focus clearly from time to time on what I believed in and kept me on the right track. Some have shared the vision, and some have carried the torch; all have, in greater and lesser parts, contributed to this book.

Martin Smith has been and continues to be a stalwart supporter of my beliefs in personal development, and has over the years encouraged my work and put up with my style of doing it.

Paul Matthews first introduced me to coaching. I was looking for something, but was not clear what it was. He gave it a name and gave it a meaning for me.

Terry Baldwin is the sort of disciple every coach needs.

John Curran gave me 'BGO'—a blinding glimpse of the obvious. Thank you John.

David Hemery and Susan Kaye shared the humorous frustration I experienced at the Ravine ('Save the Water!'), and helped me to experience coaching at first hand.

Lastly I thank the managers of Abbey National Financial Services Ltd, without whom the theory could not have turned into practice.

1 Coaching versus training

What are the differences between coaching and training? Can trainers become coaches, or is it solely the remit of the manager? This chapter defines coaching, compares the two processes and suggests a combination of both training and coaching in order to facilitate complete personal development. Also explored are the difficulties managers face with the traditional role of management in terms of target setting, and how adopting the role of coach can enhance their jobs. Furthermore, it examines the usual transformation route from subordinate to manager and proposes that the move from manager to coach can be equally daunting.

Coaching is not training

For most people the term 'coaching' has merely replaced the word training as a means of teaching or instructing people. It runs the danger of just being a new buzz word, and already I hear many trainers and managers talking about their coaching programmes, when what they really mean is their training courses. Training comes before coaching. Training is important, no more or less than coaching. Coaching follows training, it releases the skills that people have, that training alone cannot. That does not decry the use of training as a mechanism for learning. Training, as I have said, has its place, it is a starting point. People are trained to do a job in a particular way; then can be coached to do it better. The Pareto principle that 80 per cent of successful production comes from 20 per cent of the workforce is a result of the assumption that people reach the limit of their ability, that is, people reach the limit of their ability to be trained. Coaching helps people to enter a zone as yet untapped.

That untapped zone exists in what I call the performance potential iceberg (Figure 1.1). We all come to work with an existing level of knowledge, skills and attitudes. Training releases a further level, but for most people a significant mass of knowledge, skills and the attitudes which lead to successful performance remain untapped.

One of the major differences between training and coaching is that this process of determining objectives, in training terms, would be the identification of training needs. It would likewise usually be the province of trainers to decide the training needs. Yet those best placed to determine coaching needs are the people being coached. One of the main reasons why training fails so often is that there is little commitment on the part

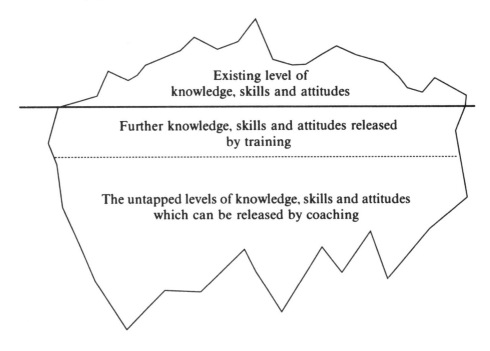

Figure 1.1 The performance potential iceberg

of the trainee. He or she may verbally agree, and take part in the training session, but emotionally few accept change, a subject covered later.

Coaching—a definition

The Manpower Services Commission in 1981 defined coaching as something which was seen as:

> Systematically increasing the ability and experience of the trainee by giving him or her planned tasks coupled with continuous appraisal advice and counselling by the trainee's supervisor.

This to me sounds like training, and while I accept that the definition is 12 years old, coaching for most people is still training by another name. As I have already said, but it bears repeating, coaching is not training. It comes *after* training.

I have defined coaching as:

> The release of latent talent and skills, previously untapped by training, through a process of self-awareness initiated by the coach.

We all have latent talent and skills. Because of circumstance and opportunity, some people are able to use some of them—most are never given the chance—or so they argue. That lack of usage, and the greater the passage of time, the less likelihood there is of that talent and skill coming to the surface. Even so, it still exists. Training can and does make use of some of our talents and skills, but only enough to complete a prescribed task. If there is a match, all well and good; if not, then the talent and skill which exist are usually lost to another company or come out in another environment. That to me is a waste. Companies spend small and even large fortunes employing people only to see them either fail completely, or simply fail to deliver previously held high expectations. I do not view this failure as the fault of individuals, at least not until they realize their complicity, but of the training process following foundation training. I make a distinction between foundation training and induction training. Foundation training is that which is given on a central course where the theory is taught. Induction is what happens on the job following foundation training. This is where the manager is meant to put the theory into practice.

One of the biggest reasons for lack of success in a role within probation is poor induction. The biggest reason for failure to supply initial high expectations can be the continuation of training when what is needed is coaching. Training teaches people to reach a standard performance. Coaching enables people to exceed the standard. Once you have delivered training and people have been given the opportunity to reach the standard, there comes a cut-off point when further training just will not work. The challenge is that that cut-off point is different for every person. That is why a blanket training programme, while adequate for the masses, falls far short for the people who may make the difference in your company—the 20 per cent who usually deliver the 80 per cent production. So how do you know when the cut-off point has been reached? A manager, working as a full-time coach, will know when it is time to move from training to coaching. Only by working with people on a one-to-one basis can a manager hope to understand what motivates an individual and what tack to take—training or coaching.

Personal responsibility for personal bests (PBs)

Inherent in the philosophy of coaching is personal ownership and responsibility. Coaching also focuses on self-awareness. Having become aware of our personal responsibility, we are also accountable for our future. We cannot change the past, but we can change the future. The instant a goal is achieved, it becomes the past. Many potential super-achievers live in the achievements of the past. POWER coaching helps the ordinary become the exceptional, and the exceptional become the extra-ordinary. Those who achieve and maintain their goals constantly seek that 'extra'—that next step.

On the day, the performance can still be *our* best. However, we can never guarantee that we will be *the* best. What we can strive for is to be the best we can be, or to be better than we have been before—to deliver a personal best (PB), whether as the person being coached or as the coach. The one thing that I have noticed with high achievers is that they are seldom satisfied with their performance. Achievers always believe that they can do better. The coach, while encouraging achievement in the individual, and emotionally rewarding it, should also be encouraging the next level of achievement. It was good to see a quotation in *The*

Times (27 February 1993) attributable to Nick Faldo, in which he is supposed to have said:

No one's so good they can't get better.

People have a basic desire to do their job well, and then to do it better. We do not all have to be the best. We do, however, need to be the best we can be. So what stops us from achieving our personal best? Perhaps part of the answer lies in the role that managers are traditionally supposed to employ with regard to setting those personal bests.

The traditional role

Traditionally managers are seen as focusing on targets. They are results orientated. Even those that are not, sometimes appear to pretend that they are, in order to be picked to play the management game and to progress. Anyone not seen to be results orientated is seen as weak. Corporate life is 'macho-management' focused. It is seen as all right to read books which focus on people, customers and quality, but on the playing field the game is tough and only the tough survive.

The traditional model for management could be represented by Figure 1.2, in which managers seek to push people from their current performance to the manager's and the company's desired performance levels. The focus for both manager and subordinate is usually always the desired performance. When people achieve goals the manager is rewarded. When people do not achieve goals the subordinate is fired. In many organizations desired performance is considerably higher than current performance. This continual focus by managers and hence subordinates on the ultimate desired performance, in itself can produce failure. Single-minded concentration on the target to the exclusion of all else is self-defeating. For most people the target can be too big to achieve. In order to keep their jobs people say they agree with the target, say they will achieve the target, and say they understand their responsibility and accountability for reaching the target. Having said that, my own field research has shown that responsibility and accountability are things which are infrequently discussed. Many recent surveys show that people at work are unclear as to the company's objectives and where they fit in. Target setting is usually an arbitrary process having already been decided some time before any manager/subordinate discussion takes place. Managers have a tendency, which is reinforced by management training, to regard forecasting and objective setting as their remit, and whether operating in a democratic fashion or not, will only occasionally involve subordinates in the process. By which time it is often too late to make any difference.

Ask your managers:

Do you decide your target, or is it decided for you by your immediate manager or even someone above them? How do you feel about that? Have you ever felt that the target was not achievable and yet still accepted it?

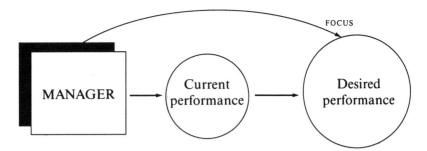

Figure 1.2 *Traditional management role*

Of greater importance:

Are discussions with your manager based on team performance, or does your manager take an interest in how you personally are performing?

By this I mean, is there a culture within the organization where managers are keen to develop the performance skills of the individuals who report to them, and not purely the job they do and the results they bring in? For example:

How would you feel, if the company you worked for was only interested in what you brought into the company and not at all interested in your own personal performance?

These questions, and the discussion they generate should gain agreement that Figure 1.2 represents for most people what actually happens. The constant focus on targets is depressing for the people who have to achieve them. It signifies an environment in which empowerment has not yet arrived. The end goal is critical to the survival of a company, but the manner in which it is reached could also have a significant influence on the future. It is reasonable to assume that most companies are set up on the basis of the long haul. They have short-term aims, but there should also be a long-term goal. Even senior executives have an interest in securing a long-term future. Yet, in day-to-day conversations with staff, managers do not refer to the future, only to the past. They spend an inordinate amount of time looking at past results and comparing them to desired performance. If both match, then all is well and the troops are left alone. If the gap is negative, then watch out. Check it out with your own managers:

What systems do you have in place to determine progress towards your targets?

I guarantee that all are based on historical data.

What can you do about the past?

If someone comes up with a viable answer, copyright it, you could make a fortune!

There is not one solitary thing that you, your managers, or the whole company can do about the past—except to learn from it. The next question you should ask is:

What has your company learnt about the way in which it has managed, trained and treated people in the past, that it should change to enhance performance in the future?

A corporate aim

A good place to start with your managers might be to determine where the company is going in terms of its aspirations, and how it is communicated to staff. Simply having a mission statement or a corporate aim is not enough: 60 per cent of companies have no corporate aim, and in those companies that do most people will not even know what it is. If you know your company has one, ask your managers to:

Write down on a piece of paper what the corporate aim is.

Very few will succeed in this task. Whether your company has a corporate aim or not a worthwhile question for discussion would be:

Is it important to have a corporate aim?

I trust in your ability to help the group decide in favour of having an aim. If you do not know where you are going you could end up somewhere else. There will be those who dispute the necessity for a corporate aim, or mission statements, and I have a great deal of sympathy with them. In too many organizations, aims and missions, and quality visions are just words. They cover gaps in the decoration rather than inspire people to work towards common objectives. People do not necessarily want to run the company, but they do want to be involved in the shape of their lives. For most people, their waking hours are spent at work, and therefore what happens at work is very important to them. Most people, given the opportunity and the correct environment, will respond to contributing to the identification of where the company is headed and how to get there. Unless people are involved in deciding the direction of the company, they will not 'buy into' the standards you impose upon them. If your own company is not achieving the standards that have been set, ask yourself whether the workforce was involved in setting the overall corporate aim and accompanying strategies. If either it was not, or you have no clear corporate aim, perhaps you should consider having one and involving the staff before going any further. Whether you push me, or pull me, I will not willingly work towards a company standard I feel I have played no part in agreeing.

Also, what about those people who arrive in the company after a corporate aim has been agreed? By arriving late on the scene, does that mean that they forgo the opportunity to contribute to the mission? Yet they will likewise be expected to reach the company standards. So, do the same rules not apply to them? Regularly update your aims by involving all staff. Ask for ideas and suggestions from staff, and share as much information with them as you can. No amount of information is too much information. Some companies will say that they have tried to involve staff, but without success. The question that needs to be asked is why? It is probably as bad as anybody who says to you:

I tried that once and it did not work.

Remember, in some cases you are attempting to undo years of poor treatment of people. Do not expect your aims to work overnight. You need to build trust before things improve, and that may take some considerable time.

Transformation of manager to coach

The most difficult thing for a manager to do is to let go of the reins of management. It makes managers uncomfortable to feel that they are not in control. The reality of the situation is that managers were never in control in the first place. Employees have traditionally allowed managers to think that they were in control simply to please them.

There are three phases (Figure 1.3, page 8) that managers will go through in the transformation from manager to coach. The symbols used represent the change of operation from the traditional managerial functions which I equate to being boxed in, through a hierarchical process of letting go, and into a more rounded approach to management—that of being a coach.

At phase 1, managers have to learn about themselves, they need to have an awareness of their true interaction with others, and you have to help them achieve this. The process of self-awareness is a painful one. Many managers will not progress past this stage, and at times you could be forgiven for doubting the existence of sufficient numbers of managers around who would willingly reduce the controls they exert. Yet, in the same way that I espouse the existence of the seed of greatness in all employees, you should understand that the same seed exists in managers. They all have it within them to succeed and to lead their teams to success. The rewards could be enormous, but for many managers the thought of letting go is terrifying. It would be like saying to someone who is frightened of water to jump in the deep end:

Don't worry—you'll be all right. It's the only way to learn!

For many managers, the transformation from manager to coach can smack too much of social work. It sounds like personnel and training theory. Managers will quickly assume that this is yet another 'flavour of the month' and that is the problem—the boy cried wolf once too often! The response could be:

Over the last decade we have been faced with one theory after another, and this is just another one but worse. In this one we are being told to let go—to stop focusing on targets, to abdicate performance responsibility, to give up controlling people. It is a veritable nightmare.

That is why going through the phases is important. Managers have first to understand what motivates them, what makes them tick, and why

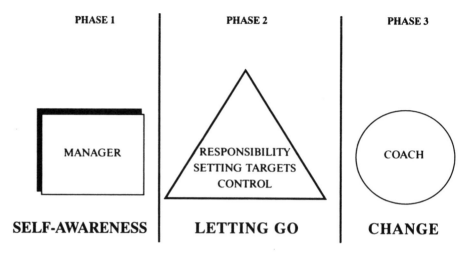

MANAGER

RESPONSIBILITY
SETTING TARGETS
CONTROL

COACH

SELF-AWARENESS   LETTING GO   CHANGE

Figure 1.3   Transformation of manager to coach

they were so keen to get into management in the first place. For many managers, the main motivation for promotion is to give up the current job, for whatever reason. For sales managers it could be a case of:

Selling's a great game so long as someone else is doing it!

In administration jobs, it can often be the case that the job is so mind-numbingly boring that the only way to get some excitement is to be a manager. The tragedy of it is that when many managers get the opportunity to change the lot of their previous peers, the stress, the boredom, and the lack of opportunity and growth are soon forgotten. For other managers one of the main reasons is to get away from the person who is their manager, to get away from being told what to do, and to be in charge—primarily of their own time.

This is important. People do not like being told what to do. Even the managers who adopt a democratic style, regularly fail to grasp that point—people do not like being told what to do. Some managers fool themselves that they democratically agree targets with their subordinates. They forget how they felt when the same game was played with them. There is no such thing as negotiating targets. The manager always knows what is required. If the subordinate starts off low, the conversation continues until the agreed target is at least at the low end of what the manager wanted anyway. The manager knows this, and the subordinate knows this. If the subordinate's offer is high, either the manager says nothing, grudgingly accepting it, or pretends to negotiate, nearly fainting with excitement as the figure goes higher and higher. And the result? Most people do not achieve their target. A further 20 per cent exceed their target by sufficient to cover those that do not meet theirs, and everybody is happy until the next time.

Throughout all of this pantomime, managers continue to look terrified most of the time as they struggle to find a way to cope. None of the theory works, none of the courses helps, not one of their peers has any better ideas than to:

Keep them focused on the target.

For the last few years I have been investigating the cause and effect of management intervention on team performance. On numerous occasions, when I proposed the question:

Why does that team succeed and that team fail?

I was frequently offered the answer:

The difference is the manager.

More recently I questioned trainers and senior managers about successful sales managers and what made them so. Suggested attributes included characteristics such as 'high expectations' and 'charisma'.

While these and similar terms constantly surface throughout the literature on management selection and development, making management training work seems ever remote. I found a disturbing number of management training programmes were evaluated either at an 'immediate reaction' level or not evaluated at all. Companies appear to spend more per head on management training than for any class of employee and yet seem unable to provide proof that the investment elicits a positive return.

Management training seems to follow fashion and fashion is sometimes dictated by the latest book. 'Customer care' replaced 'managing by wandering around' which was superseded by 'team building', which itself has been replaced by 'total quality management'. And now, it could be said, we have 'coaching'. All of these are obviously good for book sales but the question is 'Do any of them work?' There is no doubt that on paper and in the classroom the theories look attractive and yet in the field nothing seems to change. Many of the theories are attractive to senior managers, and yet in the real world it is first-line managers who carry the burden of making the theory work.

A common concern expressed to me was that productivity remains low and labour turnover high. Effective first-line managers can be counted on one hand.

Following promotion it is normal to assume that people undergo some form of metamorphosis between Friday evening and Monday morning. On Friday evening people finish work as subordinates only to wake up on Monday morning as a manager. The vast majority of managers in this country have had no formal management training, hold no recognized business qualification, and their promotion is usually based upon past performance in a subordinate role. Some, a few, are enlisted into theoretical management training events. While some of these are indeed excellent intellectual stimuli, many are devoid of practical ideas which first-line managers can use. Many courses concentrate on policy and remain at a strategic rather than operational level.

In many large companies first-line managers are left alone to develop their own styles, gaining practice through ruining subordinates' careers. Some companies are now so large that thousands of managers are able to hide within the bureaucratic machinery without being noticed.

Given that most managers have neither qualifications nor managerial achievements behind them, it is surprising how many of them continue to resist any form of training or development. Everybody, it would seem, needs training except managers. Not only are managers too busy to be trained, but most are too busy to train their own staff. The main reason why most training does not work is that managers are involved neither in its development nor in its delivery.

My research has shown that the normal criteria for selecting managers can often be irrelevant to the job that effective managers carry out. It has been said that 30 per cent of managers could be removed without it affecting the income of most companies. It would, however, have a dramatic effect on costs.

If managers are generally promoted because of past performance levels, then it seems folly not to use their knowledge and skills to coach others to the same levels of high performance. While this may seem obvious, many companies see the coaching of staff as a trainer's role and move managers into administrative functions for which most are ill-suited.

Some time ago I began working on a coaching model that placed managers directly in the driving seat of developing their teams. I moved away from the theoretical process of management towards a practical set of actions that managers could and should do each day with their staff. One of the first things I had to do was to redefine the perceived function of a manager to that of a coach.

In general terms I firmly believe in the importance of managers motivating their staff. I acknowledge that it is possible for trainers to motivate staff but that is a temporary phenomenon. The motivation induced by a trainer quickly drains away unless either the individual takes over total responsibility for self motivation, which is rare, or the manager reinforces this motivation immediately in the field.

There is another way to manage. Doing it differently and acting as coach can potentially produce significantly higher performance levels than any other form of management. It can reduce levels of stress in management, and produce the sort of working environment for everybody that has as yet not been seen in most working environments. I propose that managers give up the title 'manager' and adopt the title 'coach'. First-line managers should be 'coaches'; senior managers could be 'divisional coaches'; and head office managers and trainers should become members of the national coaching squad.

Whether this is accepted by your managers may be doubtful but why not ask them? Whatever the outcome, it is certain that too many managers operate in traditional management roles that appear to add little value to the company's performance.

Ask your managers the following questions:

1 What is the traditional role of a manager? The list produced will normally include:
   (a) an organizer
   (b) a planner
   (c) a decision maker
   (d) a delegator
   (e) a team leader
   (f) a motivator.
2 Which of these functions can either be computerized or carried out by someone in an administrative function?
3 How much of your time is spent carrying out these functions that could either be computerized or delegated to someone in an administrative function?

You will find it usual, but nevertheless disturbing, that managers spend most of their time in administration. Very little time is spent in face-to-face interaction with their employees. The longer this situation goes on, the less the manager is either willing or able to spend quality time with employees. The fact that managers themselves then contribute to the administration burden by writing to their employees, asking them to complete reports which in turn generate reams of data, which are stored on retrieval systems, which no one has the time to look at, defies belief.

The main function of a coach is to develop people's potential. Companies do have a need for managers in the traditional sense, but I would advocate that their skills may not be in the area of people management. It is indeed rare to find people who have administrative *and* people skills, and yet we seem continually to assume that in management they exist. It should not be beyond the scope of organizational development to instigate two managerial functions. Using the same headcount, it should be possible to split the traditional manager's tasks into two distinct areas—administrative and coaching—with the coaching role adopting overall accountability. In many ways, you may be able to adopt something closer to the Japanese system of management, where there are only two levels of job—managers, and employees—and yet both play on the same field. I recently saw a good departmental structure which could be worth emulating, and one which I know appears to work admirably. It is based on the structure of a football team, where the coach has adopted the role of player/coach, and the administration manager has taken the role of captain (Figure 1.4, page 12). Everyone has a clear focus on what the game is about—scoring goals. However, as the game is in progress, each person focuses on his or her role within the team. Whether they all have the same role or not is irrelevant. The player/coach's job is to motivate the staff and to work with them in a supporting role. As with football managers, the coach's job is to pick staff, to train them and to develop them. The administrative function is catered for by the captain, who is responsible for keeping the team on track, specifying and agreeing personal objectives, dealing with the administrative detail and reporting back to the coach on individual pro-

The Player/Manager determines strategy and direction.
The Captain ensures everyone is on target.

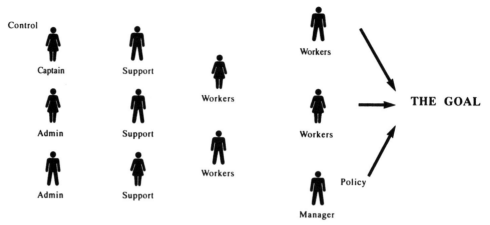

All individuals are personally responsible for their own performance, and all positions are of equal importance.

Figure 1.4   *Team structure*

gress. The captain and the coach work together in determining the success of the team. Try it with your own structure—it works.

Letting go   Phase 2 is involved in the manager letting go. Managers have to give up controlling people, give up being responsible for individual performance and give up imposing target performances. We have already covered the subject of telling, and the same thing applies to control. Nobody likes the feeling of being controlled.

A simple example is to place a manager inside a circle of peers, having told the individual to go to one area of the room and the group surrounding to go to the other. The individual is instructed to fold his or her arms, but the group can use any means at their disposal to move the individual to the other side of the room. Then ask the group what similarities there are between this exercise and the working environment. Some of the learning points to come out should be:

• People are sometimes surrounded by rules.
• It is rare for staff and managers to have to play by the same rules.
• Communication at times seems contradictory.
• Being controlled, leaves the individual feeling helpless and resentful.

I have also touched briefly on the subject of personal responsibility and it is an important area to drive home. The coach cannot be responsible for the performance of the individual, only for his or her own performance. If the individual fails to deliver personal potential performance on the day, and yet in practice appeared capable of doing so, and was seen to be capable of doing so, then the coach cannot be responsible for failure. Yet many managers assume personal failure in the failure of their subordinates, as though it were possible to shoulder blame just because they hold the manager position. It is a fine balance. The other side of the coin is those managers who constantly refuse to accept their accountability. The manager is not responsible for failure to deliver performance if he or she:

1 provided the individual with sufficient support when it was needed
2 reached full agreement on areas of personal responsibility
3 provided the individual with sufficient feedback in order to determine the true likelihood of executing the task.

An example from the athletic world is, that having coached someone to a record-breaking time in practice, and subsequently the same record-breaking time was delivered on the track, how responsible could the coach be if another athlete delivered a faster time? Obviously, what other people do cannot be dictated. Perhaps planned for, but not dictated, and certainly not coached for. Also, what personal responsibility could the coach have if the athlete tripped during the race? Obviously none. What about in a work environment then? If a person had been coached to deliver a performance in a negotiation situation, and someone else delivered a better performance, what personal responsibility should the coach shoulder? The same answer applies—none. In business as in sport, the coach may ultimately be accountable. In sport the coach may not take his or her team to the Olympics. In business the individual may be beaten at the negotiation table and subsequently the firm and the coach may suffer. That accountability goes with the job. The problem is that many managers confuse responsibility with accountability. Responsibility is a personal thing and can only be attached to those things over which you have direct control.

Sometimes for the best reasons, most times because it is easier and quicker, managers take on board personal responsibility for completing the task, either by telling people specifically what to do, or by doing part of the whole task themselves. It is normal, when the manager is absent, for the task to be completed to a greater level of efficiency by the team, who enjoy the freedom to express themselves free from interference. The other possibility is that the task is not completed at all. Each person is responsible for his or her own job.

Targets

From all that I have said so far, it may appear that the obvious person to set the target is the individual. It may seem somewhat contradictory, but I believe that target setting is the remit of the company. By the target, what I mean is that the company sets out what has to be achieved. By letting go however, what I mean is that just because the company sets a target performance, there is no guarantee that it is either achievable by the vast majority of people employed or that each individual will, even if capable, reach it. Psychologically, each person, in order to achieve someone else's goal, has to accept the goal personally.

Set up two dart boards, and split the management group on the event into two teams. Elect two team leaders, and separately tell each team leader that the target the team has to reach is to throw a dart into each number on the board, whether single, double or treble does not matter. The team leaders have to organize the team in such a way that everyone throws a dart in rotation, no one can be missed out. In this way, even if one member of the team is an expert at the game, he or she has to wait for a turn to throw again. The difference in instructions is that one team ('A') has to hit the numbers in a sequence you prescribe to the manager, who in turn prescribes it number by number to the team. The other team leader (team 'B') is told that the team can hit their numbers in any sequence, and that the team leader's task is merely to encourage effort and achievement.

After team 'B' wins, which inevitably they will, debrief the group.

The first thing that will happen is that team 'A' will say that they were given a different set of rules, and that team 'B' won because they were given the freedom to hit any number. The end result was therefore an unfair reflection of their ability. The learning points are:

1 On random selection of teams, it would be usual for the teams to be of equal ability.
2 Both teams were given the same target—to hit all numbers.
3 Those given freedom in how to reach the target will usually do so quicker and more effectively, and with greater enthusiasm.
4 Freedom, coupled with a step-by-step approach dictated by the individual, will inevitably result in higher achievement levels than prescribed actions and steps. Even if the end result had not been reached, which seems doubtful, each person's sense of achievement from setting a personal target within an overall objective, makes for a more enjoyable and meaningful team effort.

A further stage that you could employ here, is once team 'B' had completed the task, to ask them whether they could do it again, but faster, while team 'A' was still trying to complete the first run. Also, let them set their own time, having already timed them on the first run. You will find that they will usually achieve the second run faster, sometimes even within the same period that team 'A' struggles to complete its task. Those given a freedom to compete at their own pace and direction will deliver a performance of higher quality and quantity than those directed to do so.

Everyone should know what is expected of him or her, and many people given the opportunity will set for themselves far higher goals than the company target. Constant focus on the company target is self-defeating. The role of coach is through a changing of attitude towards managing individuals to move to a position of pulling people towards a desired performance (Figure 1.5) by helping the individual to focus on the next step, rather than focusing on the company's target performance. The surprising thing is, by refocusing on the next step, the company's

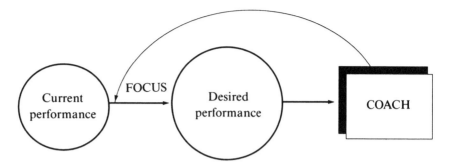

Figure 1.5 *New model of the manager as coach*

desired performance levels are reached quicker, and surpassed more often. This represents the change from traditional management practice to suggested coaching and completes the third phase as shown in Figure 1.3.

Motivational theory and management style

Motivational theory has occupied space on business bookshelves for most of the century. In reality the search for what motivates people to achieve probably began with the Greeks, and has continued unabated to the present day. Most people will have studied the theories of Maslow and Hertzberg, both of which in many ways encompass dissatisfaction with what went before, in that managers believed that people produced effort solely for extrinsic reward. There were, however, theorists that concluded that internal factors such as the need for self-worth, sense of achievement and fulfilment were of greater relevance to self-motivation.

The traditional model of motivation, referred to sometimes as the scientific model, held that management's role was: (a) to find the right quality of worker for the task in hand; (b) to train them effectively to do the job required; and (c) to install a financial reward system geared to workers maximizing their income by doing what was expected of them. The theory rested on the premiss that most workers were basically lazy, dishonest, lacked direction and were mercenary. In other words 'theory X'.

A cornerstone of coaching philosophy can be summed up by Douglas McGregor's theory of management contained in his book *The Human Side of Enterprise*. It should form part of your own reading and belief. McGregor believed that managers were ultimately responsible for the performance of companies, and that the assumptions that they had about human behaviour dictated the way in which people performed for them. In his theory X he described managers who believed that workers generally dislike work, are only motivated by reward, have to be closely supervised, have little ambition, and lack creativeness and initiative. It has been interesting to conduct management training sessions where, when I display theory X on a flip chart I can usually guarantee that a large number of managers will empathize with the theory. I then go on to explain McGregor's 'Y' theory which is that for most people work is as natural as play, people do not have to be constantly directed to achieve, creativity is equally distributed throughout the population, people are as interested in intrinsic reward as they are in extrinsic, and large numbers of people are keen to accept personal responsibility. Even after giving managers theory Y many remain sceptical.

For your own sanity, you should seek to reinforce your own belief in theory Y. Like you, McGregor believed that people were capable of far greater performance levels than probably they had hitherto achieved. While McGregor's theories are not the panacea that he would have originally wished, they do form a foundation stone upon which to build your own coaching philosophy. In sharing the theory with managers, be sure that your own style, with your own staff, reflects the style you advocate your managers to adopt.

A useful way to teach the theory, alongside that just described, is to split the group into two teams: 'A' and 'B'. Give them the following briefs:

Team 'A'
You are to prepare for a debate with team 'B' defending your belief that:

1 The average human being has an inherent dislike of work and will avoid it if they can.
2 Because of this dislike, most people have to be coerced, directed, controlled, or threatened, in order that they exert enough energy to achieve the task.
3 The average human being prefers to be directed, wants to avoid responsibility, has relatively little ambition, and above all else wants security.

Team 'B'
You are to prepare for a debate with team 'A' who will be presenting an argument which is contrary to your belief that:

1 For the vast majority of people, work is as natural as play.
2 Managerial control or threats are not the only way to get things done. People will achieve goals under their own steam and will commit themselves to the task given the opportunity to do so.
3 Money is not the only motivator, people get reward from having achieved a goal.
4 Under the right conditions, the average human will seek out and accept responsibility.
5 Initiative and creativity are widely distributed among the population.
6 Companies use only a fraction of the potential of their employees.

You chair the debate, allowing each side to put its point of view, and then permit the other team to question their propositions.

What is interesting is that, even if some of the people in team 'B' do not initially agree with their brief, they will support it to the end, and that fact alone is worthy of discussion.

Having therefore stimulated debate on some of the differences between the internal beliefs and perceptions of managers, the next stage is to develop discussion on what makes a good coach.

Summary

- Coaching and training are not the same. Each complements the other.
- The major differences between coaching and training are that the coach does not set the training agenda; each performer accepts personal responsibility for the items in his or her remit that he or she can perform; the focus is on personal bests 'PBs' and not on the target.
- The traditional role of managers setting performance goals for subordinates is at odds with the role of the coach.
- Managers adopting coaching as a principal activity have to stop telling people what to do.
- The normal criteria for selecting managers appear to produce managers who are not best suited to coaching roles.
- Many of the traditional managerial responsibilities can be computerized.

Recommended reading

McGregor, Douglas (1960) *The Human Side of Enterprise.* McGraw-Hill.
McGregor, Douglas (1966) *Leadership and Motivation.* MIT Press.
McGregor, Douglas (1967) *The Professional Manager.* McGraw-Hill.

2 Attributes of a good coach

The attributes and skills required by the coach are discussed, as is motivational theory and management style.

So what are the attributes and skills required by a coach? When asked this question, managers themselves have come up with the following list:

- Caring skills
- Observation skills
- Questioning skills
- Supportive skills
- Listening skills
- Verbal skills
- Non-verbal skills
- Counselling ability
- Patience
- Awareness

Employees asked the same question tend to come up with a remarkably similar list. I intend to focus on the small number that I believe makes the difference in coaching, and to share with you some ideas on how to improve them.

Listening skills

It has been said that in an average working day people spend 9 per cent of the time writing, 16 per cent of the time reading, 30 per cent of the time speaking, and an astonishing 45 per cent of the time listening to other people. I say astonishing, because if you think about how much time we were allocated at school and in further education to learn how to write, read, and speak, and compare that to how time was devoted to learning how to listen, perhaps we can begin to understand why we are so bad at listening to each other.

Managers have a firm belief that they have little time available for all the things they have to do. This perception of the pressure they are under contributes to poor listening skills. One of the more common complaints that employees have of their managers is:

They just don't listen.

Ask your own managers:

What were you taught about listening?

The answer will be nothing. So if that is the case, teaching listening skills should be a prime requisite of any training event concerned with the personal development of communication skills.

Listening skills test Ask your managers to complete the listening test shown in Table 2.1.

Table 2.1 *Listening skills test*

Question	Yes	No
1. When you attend a conference, do you aim to sit at the front?		
2. At meetings, do you take notes and then read them up later?		
3. When you are listening to somebody do you ask questions to clarify your understanding?		
4. Do you sometimes daydream when people are talking to you?		
5. Have you ever had somebody say to you 'You're not listening to me'?		
6. When you are listening to somebody do you sit so that you can see the facial expressions of the speaker?		
7. Are you an excellent listener?		
8. If someone is saying something you disagree with, do you let the speaker finish before interrupting?		
9. Can you remember all the conversations you had yesterday?		
10. Do you only listen to attractive people or people who have superiority over you?		
11. Can you empathize with other people's point of view even though it can be radically different to yours?		
12. Do you encourage people when they are speaking to you by nodding, looking at them attentively, and reviewing with them what they have said to you?		
13. Can you list at least five barriers to effective listening?		
14. Can you remember a time when someone new was speaking to you and you couldn't remember his or her name?		
15. Do you need to develop your listening skills?		

Rather than marking the papers and ending up with a score, discuss with the group the answers each person gave. In some cases you should expand on the answer. For example if the answer given to No. 11 is 'Yes', ask them to explain how they are able to show this empathy. Likewise, if No. 7 is answered yes, ask how.

Barriers to effective listening include:

- Being tired
- Being preoccupied with another problem
- Disagreeing with the speaker
- Disliking the speaker, for whatever reason
- External noise or distractions
- Feeling physically uncomfortable
- Thinking ahead

There could obviously be others. Get your managers to brainstorm as many as possible. Each is worthy of discussion.

The effect of not being listened to

In order to help the group to appreciate what it feels like not to be listened to you could expose them to the following training.

Prior to the event, do not tell people what the content of the session is to be. Arrange the group into a circle. Pick a subject, any subject, for discussion. Allow each person in the circle to make a comment, in a clockwise order, no more than one minute about the topic. Once the full circle has spoken, ask the second person who spoke what the first person said. Ask the same question of all participants, going around the circle, again in a clockwise fashion. It will not take long to go round the circle again. Most will have forgotten what the previous person said, or simply not paid attention in the first place. Ask each person what it felt like not to be listened to.

Pick another subject, or better still allow participants to pick their own subject, something which they can talk about for no more than one minute. Ask each person to speak, going around the circle in a clockwise order. After each person has spoken, ask the person to the right of the first speaker to recall what that speaker said, and continue the process in an anticlockwise order. The chances are, that most will be unable to respond.

Discuss the reasons for this, and again ask people what it was like not to be listened to. One point you may want to bring out is, that having learnt to play the game the first time around, most people were locked into one process, which had a personal pay-off. That pay-off will have had more to do with attempting to avoid personal embarrassment, rather than really listening.

Begin again with the first speaker, who should tell the group something about themselves. At random, then pick someone to repeat what the speaker said. After which, ask the speaker whether the résumé was a fair reflection of what had been said. You need to keep a tally-sheet going, as you should use a similar process for each person to speak, and to feed back.

Once again, this exercise will provide you with a considerable number of discussion points, and also feedback from individuals on how it now felt to be listened to.

Repeat the last item, but instruct the person reviewing to ask the speaker three questions about himself or herself before feeding back.

The ensuing discussion should bring out how much better you feel when people ask you questions about yourself, and how good it feels to be listened to by someone who appears interested.

Messages get distorted

The classic listening skills exercise is 'Chinese Whispers'.

Type up the following on a piece of paper:

Your boss has arranged a meeting in Darlington which will begin at 4.00 p.m. He cannot make the beginning, so he wants you to start the meeting without him. You will have to pick up a parcel on the 3.00 p.m. through train which will be addressed to you, the contents of which should be handed out five minutes prior to starting the meeting. Ask everybody to spend ten minutes completing the questionnaire contained in the parcel, then leave it to one side while you get on with the month's results. Tell them that the boss will be there at around 4.30 p.m.

Ask everyone to leave the room except one person. Repeat the above message to this person, and tell him or her to ask the next person to come in and repeat the same message.

If you keep a tally-sheet you will see that, before long, large items contained within the message will be lost or changed.

Non-verbal skills

Ideally, coaches should be interested in the development of others, but failing that, it is just as important to look interested. Good coaches get as much response from people by not saying anything, rather than by saying too much. Coaches need a strong knowledge and understanding of body language. I recommend that aspiring coaches read as much as they can about the subject, and receive as much training in body language as time and resource can afford.

We already know that non-verbal language represents 60–80 per cent of communication. It seems asinine to ignore the fact. Yet most managers pay it little regard, apart from late-night sessions of charades, and strutting postures at meetings and conferences.

Two areas in particular that I recommend you focus on are the areas of facial expression and of touch.

Facial expression

We learn by seeing. In excess of 70 per cent of all information we take in is through visual stimulus. We cannot see words, only pictures. That is why it is important to learn how to paint pictures in people's minds. Learning to communicate visually is vital. We do it anyway, whether we are aware of it or not. The problem is that if there is a discrepancy between what we say and what we show by our face or body posture, people will always believe what we show.

Prepare a set of cards and write a single word on each card as follows:

- Fear
- Anger
- Sympathy
- Sadness
- Happiness
- Pride
- Encouragement
- Interest

Write the words on a flip chart. One by one, ask managers to come forward, receive a card and display the attribute or gesture written on it. You will need to get people to focus on an event in their mind that made them feel the sensation you are asking them to display.
For example:

Think of a time when you were last angry. Take a few seconds to think the thing through in your head before you show your colleagues a facial expression of that feeling.

The others then simply write down what they perceive the emotion or attribute is. Carry on with this exercise until you see improvement, which will be apparent with time.

Pick some book or film titles, and have the group play facial charades. They have to act out the book, using facial expressions only. They cannot speak other than telling people when they are cold, warm, or hot. Some ideas for titles could include:

- *The Compleat Angler*
- *The Karma Sutra*
- *The Longest Day*
- *Batman*
- *Alien*
- *Developing Managers as Coaches*!

Touching   Touching is something nobody gets trained in, and yet it is an important function of communication. It has been shown that tactile people are more likely to be liked than non-tactile people. Having said that, touch is also a matter of culture. In the United Kingdom touching can sometimes be seen as a taboo—'This person is invading my personal space!' Yet in places like France, Italy and Germany, touching between consenting adults is very acceptable, especially in areas like greetings. In Germany, if you fail to shake hands when you meet someone, it could be construed as being stand-offish, and in some circles extremely rude. A colleague of mine originally came from Cyprus, and to watch him communicate is a real pleasure to behold. His personality is extremely outgoing anyway, but in common with many Latins he has a noticeable habit of using his hands to communicate, and is very tactile. His effect on the stereotypical British workplace environment is dramatic. On meeting he embraces people, both men and women, with a gusto that starts each day off on the right note. At the beginning, I was concerned when I observed him throw his arms around a female colleague of mine to wish her good morning—someone he hadn't seen for a few days. She later told me when I asked if she minded:

Mind? It's the greatest start to the day I've had since coming to work here!

Before you take this on board however, I should also warn you that I received complaints from two other female members of staff who felt intimidated by his behaviour—as in all things, you cannot please all of the people all of the time!

If you body-watch, like I do, it is fascinating how most people avoid being touched, and yet those that engage in tactile behaviour look far less repressed and more open. It is the last bit—openness—that I want to focus on here.

It is important when building a coaching relationship to establish open behaviour—openness in terms of what can be said to each other, and just as important for the individual being touched, what can be attempted. A coach will often encourage the individual to try things he or she may not have tried before, and therefore run the potential risk of looking and acting foolish. Unless a completely open relationship has been established, then the individual will feel reticent about trying something new. Touching is merely one additional part of a total communication system that coaches can employ to help them establish a supportive relationship with the person being coached. Touching is therapeutic, and supportive. It is comforting and encouraging, and used correctly can enhance positive communication. Used properly it will also not be noticed by the person being touched.

I am not suggesting every reader adopts the 'Latin' approach; it may conflict with our natural behaviour. But as with all things there is some value in adopting some of the behaviour.

It is vitally important that on each meeting the coach shakes hands. It breaks into the personal space, and immediately establishes a close working relationship. Likewise, shake hands when parting, and if possible reinforce the handshake with a light touch on the elbow. Accompanied by a supporting verbal message, about the worth of the individual, or an encouraging message about carrying out some practice while the coach is away, it will add value to the message. The handshake need not be a bone-cruncher, but it should be firm. Get managers to practise shaking hands with each other, and to feed back what their handshakes feel like. Determine what feels good, and what feels weak. The ideal handshake should be firm, and straight.

Touching the elbow when giving a verbal message adds credibility to the message. Ask managers to say something to each other in pairs, once without touching and once with an accompanying light touch on the elbow. Then ask them which statement made them feel more comfortable. It will invariably be the statement accompanied with the touch. Get them to practise this touch so that it is light, not forced, and barely noticeable. This elbow touch should be used sparingly—only when you really want to emphasize something.

The two other places to touch are the upper arm at the back, and preferably the back of the shoulder—either one. It is simply back-slapping. Congratulating people for a task well done, or an attempt at something new. Two light taps are sufficient. Once again, you should encourage managers to practise until they are comfortable at giving these light supportive touches.

Even better, would be for you to record yourself during an earlier session, walking round the group of managers, encouraging them, and lightly touching when applicable. You could then show them what had happened, and I can guarantee that most will not have noticed, but will have felt encouraged.

Jane Lyle quotes an experiment in a university library where an assistant was asked to lightly touch the hands of some students returning books, and not others. Those touched scored both the assistant and the library higher, than those not touched.

Observation skills

Nothing drives home the problems associated with individual perception, and the difficulties of acquiring consistent observation skills than a recruitment selection centre. It is rare to find two managers, watching the same person being interviewed, who will have the same views, or even it would seem, see the same performance. Yet good observation skills are a vital component of good coaching. The coach has to be objective in feedback of performance, and as such has to be able to help the person being coached recall specifically any item which requires attention. The best way to instil this skill is through repetition of an observation exercise, and practice.

Record an interview on video, and play it back to a group of managers. Each manager should present his or her opinions without examples and without discussion first. Write each manager's opinion of the candidate on a separate piece of flip chart and put the charts on the wall. It is guaranteed that there will be discrepancies, many of them major. Then ask each manager to justify his or her opinion by quoting examples of behaviour. The other managers are then allowed to contribute their own feelings. Each point of dispute should eventually be reviewed by playing the video interview at the appropriate point.

You may need a bank of video interviews so that this process can be repeated a number of times, each time improving the skills of the group. The main points to derive from this should be:

- Clear criteria against which to judge the candidate
- Simple but precise note taking
- No judgement without examples

Following this exercise you can repeat it using people performing their job.

Questioning skills

The art of questioning is the key element in the process. Chapter 6 covers as much as your managers need to know about the type of questions they should be asking. Together with the section in this chapter on listening skills, I believe that they should be well prepared to be a coach. It does take significant practice however. As with much training that goes on, failure to practise the newly acquired knowledge or skill will quickly erode that knowledge and skill.

Verbal skills

It is how you say it, not what you say. Give managers a simple sentence like:

I did not say you broke the vase.

Going round the circle, ask each speaker to alter the meaning of the sentence, by placing a greater emphasis on a particular word. There are at least seven variations. The point is that the meaning changes with the emphasis. How many managers train in voice modulation? Very few. Besides, non-verbal language, I consider voice tone and control to be a vital constituent part of effective managerial communication. This has nothing to do with grammar or accent, it has to do with delivery, and everyone can learn to deliver lines better through practice.

A good way to prove the point is to take a section from a famous speech, something from Shakespeare will do. I recently used a section of the 'Dream Speech' by Martin Luther King. It should be something that people can get their teeth into. Give the speech to one of the delegates a few weeks before the training event, and ask him or her to learn it. Send the speech to another delegate a week before the event. Give a copy of the speech to another delegate on the first morning of the event, having decided to schedule the speech-making either at the end of the day, or the next day. Lastly, ask someone without notice to read the speech out, followed in the reverse order by the people that you gave copies to. The difference is always noticeable and sometimes dramatic.

If you can, pick the one you gave the speech to first with greater care than the rest. What you are looking for is an extrovert. I know it may be stacking the deck in your favour, but everyone can lean to act like an extrovert, your problem on most courses is that you do not have enough time.

Another way to do this is to pick a paragraph from a story in the newspaper, and ask each person to read it out in turn, giving each one a different expression such as sounding angry, sad, happy, apprehensive, superior, defensive, proud, etc. The others have to guess the emotion.

Then again, try picking a really sad story from the paper, and have someone sing it out loud to the tune of 'The Sun Has Got His Hat On'! It sort of spoils the effect of the story, but it could reinforce what is it you are trying to impart.

Counselling skills

Counselling can be said to be a process whereby the counsellor helps an individual talk about, and solve, either a real or a perceived problem, and assists the individual to make a decision with regard to a course of action. In coaching, there are no problems, only opportunities. The course of action is essentially up to that individual, but the coach may have to direct when appropriate. There are many who believe that managers should not counsel their own subordinates. Potentially the best and most effective counsellor is the manager. All managers have a responsibility to counsel their staff in terms of their performance. People have a basic desire to know how they are performing and to have the opportunity of discussing their performance concerns and aspirations with the manager. People generally have a basic desire to do their job better.

Coaching and counselling seek to increase self-esteem of the individual; both accept that the individual's personal feelings are more important than perceived logical solutions; both the counsellor and the coach need to have an understanding of human nature and psychology; and both ultimately seek to help the individual to change. Counselling requires the manager to display a set of communication skills which help people to manage their own performance issues by using their own resources.

Everyone has the potential to solve his or her own performance issues, and to perform at the highest levels.

As I have said before, a great deal depends on self-awareness, and counselling can help people to determine where they are, where it is they want to be and how to get there. Coaching helps people, once having decided on a course, to put decisions into practice. In this way it is possible to help people change and increase the levels of their knowledge, skills and attitudes.

Summary

- Coaches are caring, supportive and patient; they have good listening skills and are as much aware of their own strengths and weaknesses as those of their teams; they have good verbal and non-verbal skills and are good observers and counsellors.
- Managers becoming coaches should be exposed to some 'self-awareness' training in order to experience the special needs of those being coached.
- Of the skills required of good coaches, probably the most difficult to acquire is that of good observation. Managers, and trainers, are all too often guilty of cutting short training and coaching sessions by their eagerness to interrupt.

Recommended reading

Argyle, Michael (1972) *The Psychology of Interpersonal Behaviour*, Penguin.

Burley-Allen, Madelyn (1982) *Listening: The Forgotten Skill*. John Wiley & Sons.

Clark, Neil and Fraser, Tony (1987) *The Gestalt Approach*. Roffey Park Institute.

Couper, David and Stewart, Jacqueline (1993) *25 Role Plays for Developing Counselling Skills*. Gower.

Lyle, Jane (1990) *Body Language*. Reed International.

Megranahan, Mike (1985) 'Counselling at work', *Journal of General Management*, **11** (1), Autumn.

Rogers, C. (1961) *On Becoming a Person*. Houghton Mifflin.

Stanton, Nicki (1982) *Communication*. Macmillan.

Stewart, Ian (1989) *Transactional Analysis Counselling in Action*. Sage Publications.

3 Developing management awareness of the benefits of coaching

This chapter shows how important it is to sell the whole concept of coaching to managers. Yet if the coaching philosophy is to be followed, managers themselves have to produce the benefits associated with coaching. The chapter covers how to do this and provides the trainer with a list of useful discussion points.

Good managers and bad managers

While most managers will agree that coaching is important, the vast majority do not do any. The gap between theory and practice is never more present than that in management responsibility for staff development. In the late 1980s the emphasis on who was responsible for staff development moved from central trainers to field work by the line manager. Yet if you conduct a survey of the workforce in any company, at any level, I guarantee that you will find that the least involved person in staff development is the line manager. It is a paradox that managers continually agree to the theory, but rarely practise it.

You can help managers focus on the contradictory nature of management theory and practice by asking them to do the following exercise:

Write down in detail the attributes of a good manager you have worked for, focusing in particular on what he or she did, and how he or she behaved.

It is likely that the list will contain some or all of the following items:

- Behaves positively
- Shows mutual respect
- Reviews progress
- Gives feedback
- Has experience of the job well done
- Leads by example
- Makes people feel valued
- Decision maker
- Accountable
- Available
- Visible

Then ask the same managers to describe the attributes of a bad manager they have worked for. This list will probably contain the following items:

- Shows self-interest
- Autocratic
- Tells
- Criticizes
- Never satisfied
- Does not accept responsibility
- Fails to encourage
- Takes all credit for success
- Blames others for failure
- Fails to give motivation
- Never praises

Then ask them which manager they all strive to be. All of them should agree to endeavour to be the good manager. If anyone does not, get on to personnel and start the exit process! Then lead the discussion on to which type of manager they tend to be most of the time. This is very much an honesty session, and it depends on the relationship between the trainer and the group how honest people will be. My experience is that many management courses tend to be like confessionals, and managers do open up to their failings. They, like their subordinates, are concerned, when given the opportunity, to improve their performance.

Most will admit that when in the field, they probably display the attributes contained on the bad manager list.

Why is this, and why is the problem so common? I have spoken to a number of senior managers, most of whom espouse all of the attributes of the items in the good manager list, and also believe sincerely in the role of manager as coach. Yet, in practice, they find their middle managers either unable or unwilling to employ coaching, and complain of managers who:

Just don't seem to act like we want them to.

Quite often I hear senior managers say of their first-line managers:

I simply don't know where they learnt how to behave like that—I certainly didn't show them that way of managing.

The problem is, that they probably did. In the same way that first-line managers have difficulty practising what they preach, the memory of senior managers tends to become very rosy with the passing of time.

The main reason usually given for failing to employ coaching in the field is 'lack of time', when in reality the main reason is likely to be that the organization does not have a coaching philosophy. It might be contained in a training mission statement; senior managers might be rolled out to attend training sessions to lend support to the theory; they might actually write sections in the training manual supporting coaching; however, as with all things to do with managers, people are influenced by how managers behave, not by what they say. Also, there are many organizations and many managers who still believe that the training of the workforce is the job of the trainer. They may not express that opinion, and may actually say that they support coaching. Indeed, in any organization which is spending considerable sums of money introducing a coaching system, it may be politically damaging to voice dissent. Managers and staff alike know that in the long run coaching will be replaced by something else, and everyone will be able to return to the *status quo*.

What are the benefits of coaching?

So why introduce coaching anyway? The benefits of coaching are numerous and are enumerated below.

The employee performs the job better

Over a period of time, people tend to perform to a level that they feel comfortable at. In some companies it meets the standards of performance expected. In others it falls short of the mark, but not so much as to alert managers that something radical has to be done. From my experience, companies elicit a level of performance from their employees which represents a fraction of what people are capable of.

Next time you have a group of trainees together, it could be enlightening for you to ask them to describe what they do in their spare time. I have heard the following list:

• Writing a book
• Building a boat
• Running marathons
• Captaining a football team
• Leading a community project
• Being a magistrate
• Studying for a degree

All of which show me quite clearly that millions of people face greater challenges, derive more satisfaction and gain a far higher sense of achievement outside of work than inside. The disturbing thing is that these achievements are not driven by reward. People receive no pay for much of this activity, but satisfy an internal want that many people have which remains unfulfilled at work.

Many employees, when away from the workplace, are able to express themselves in ways which the company seems either not to be aware of, or appears incapable of tapping into. In terms of talent and skill, and their application, people are generally held back by managerial practices more suited to the army than to the needs of corporate Britain.

Employees working in a true coaching environment, where the focus is on personal development, rather than the accomplishment of the task, find a stimulus which results in a more effective task completion. Focus on the elements which make up a person's performance, together with the coaching principles outlined in this book, can result and has resulted in higher performance levels.

It would be a useful exercise for you to keep track of some of the things that employees do in their spare time. When you get the managers together, without divulging names, find out whether they are aware of any projects that their staff are working on outside of work.

Set your managers the following task:

On your own, write down, in your experience, what things prevent people from performing to a higher level than they are now.

The ensuing discussion will be useful. Focus with them on the things that they can personally do in terms of their relationships with their people. When I conducted my own survey with staff to whom I asked the question:

What is stopping you from achieving more than you are now?

The top answers in order were:

1 My boss
2 Lack of training
3 No incentive
4 Lack of help
5 Too much emphasis on teamwork
6 Pressure from the boss
7 Lack of financial reward
8 No back-up
9 Too much paperwork
10 Target performance not achievable

When I asked managers what they believed they could do to get the best out of people they said:

- Training—15 per cent
- Leading by example—20 per cent
- Supporting—30 per cent
- Setting goals—45 per cent
- Motivating—60 per cent
- Ensuring reward—65 per cent
(multiple choices answers)

Managers still have a firm belief that people are motivated by reward and incentive, when in reality, incentives and reward that result in sustained high achievement come from within. Recent research has shown that the main job motivators for increased performance are:

- Satisfaction of job well done
- Increased chances of promotion
- Achievement of targets
- Satisfaction of customer needs
- Effort acknowledged
- Make more money

- Meet my family responsibilities
- Improve my lifestyle
- Satisfy my manager's expectations

I can also guarantee that each time you run a management training event and ask the same question, you will always come up with different answers.

Therefore, a worthwhile question to pose to your managers is:

If we keep coming up with different answers to the question what motivates people to perform better, who has the right answer?

In truth, it is each individual, and that is where POWER coaching comes into its own. It enables each individual to vocalize with his or her manager, what personal motivation is required to deliver his or her best performance level.

A better relationship is formed between manager and employee

Whichever way you look at it, people do not like being managed. They do not like being told what to do, controlled, instructed, manipulated, or experimented on by the latest management fad. Coaching runs the risk of being the latest in a long line of management fads.

Ask any group of managers:

Why did you want to become a manager?

The chances are that something along the lines of:

I wanted to be responsible for managing my own time,

or

I wanted to be in control,

or something similar will emerge. Then ask:

What was there about being a non-manager that you didn't like?

Inevitably:

Being told what to do

will surface. The next question should be:

So why is it that when most of you become managers, the first thing you do is to seek to control people, and start telling them what to do?

It is a contradiction that many will be unable to answer, and yet the answer is simple enough. We grow up being told what to do by our parents and relatives. We attend school where we are told what to do. Society, and the existence of a structured set of rules which govern us, tell us how to behave. Arrival at work, where many of us expect to be treated as adults, is dampened by managers telling us what to do. By the time we get to be managers ourselves, the constant exposure to telling as a means to elicit action is so ingrained that we begin telling others what to do.

The problem that many managers will face in implementing a coaching ethos, is that many believe that you have to be one type of manager. What I mean by this is that managers, new managers especially, struggle to find a style which works, and having learnt one, or fallen into a trait, find it difficult to adopt another:

You want me to be responsible for these objectives, and at the same time abdicate control to the individual—the two do not go together.

Managers are no different to anyone else, they just happen to have job titles that include the word 'manager'. I would like to see a company brave enough to call its managers 'coaches', and then perhaps we might see a change of behaviour. Were you to suggest this, however, the hue and cry from existing managers would be heard from John-o'-Groat's to Land's End. Managers like to tell their friends that they are a manager. Trying to explain what a coach is, is beyond most, and even perhaps beyond our culture anyway.

In my experience, many managers struggle with their relationships with employees. Knowing what it feels like to be managed, seems not to register when they themselves become managers. Everyone, employees and managers alike, is looking for the answer, the only constant being that managers and employees are different, or so they think. Clearly they cannot be. Managers are not born, they are promoted from the ranks of employees. That act of promotion, however, triggers in many managers a change of behaviour which in itself alienates them from people with whom they used to work. Granted, the employee also begins to behave differently towards a former colleague who has been promoted, but perhaps this has more to do with an expectation of change and a perception of what managers usually do. It is quite usual for employees to voice the opinion:

Oh her, she's changed completely now she's a manager. Used to be one of us. Acquired airs and graces now.

In some ways it could be the self-fulfilling prophesy. That expectation of change of behaviour in both parties' reaction to each other, can actually produce a change. Yet the relationship should be enhanced if approached correctly, not deteriorate. Surely, the newly promoted manager should have a greater sense of oneness with former colleagues? In many cases it would seem not.

Adopting the role of coach can and does help. The difficulty is, as I have already said, that many managers see coaching as a soft option. Sales managers, especially, see coaching as an abdication of management. You have probably heard the phrase:

Management reserves the right to manage.

And so they should. Coaching to me is simply another tool in the armoury, which managers can and should employ when the situation demands it. The predicament is that managers fear letting go. They see coaching as releasing control—they say they understand it, fail to use it, and then are unable to apply it when the time and situation demand. Any skill which is unused deteriorates. It is quite usual for managers to say:

I know how to do it—it's just that it isn't appropriate most of the time.

If you still have the dartboard up in the training room, from a session in the last chapter, simply ask the group:

Who knows how to score 50 on the dartboard with one dart?

Most will obviously know that the Bull's Eye scores 50. Then ask:

So what do you have to do with the dart to get a result of 50 with one dart?

The skill is in throwing the dart at the right height, with the right force, in the right direction, and with practice it can be learnt. Now get each manager to throw one dart and ask them to score 50. One in a hundred will do it. The learning point is that they all know what to do, but because they do not practise the skill regularly, the vast majority will not be able to do it. Similarly, just because managers know how to do something, simply telling others *what* to do is no guarantee that others can do it. Exercises like this are merely a means of developing self-awareness, as is the next sequence.

Ask your managers:

1 What sort of relationship do you want to have with the people you work with?

A point worth focusing on here is the practice of managers referring to people as 'my people', 'my team', 'my staff', and the need to change their behaviour on this. As a supplementary question, before they answer No. 1 say:

1(a) You'll notice that I said 'the people you work with', as opposed to 'your team', or 'your people'. Is there something about these phrases that is important? For example, how do you think the people you work with react when you call them 'your' team, or 'your' people?

The response to these questions can produce interesting discussion points. Some managers will find it hard to understand. Some may not realize the condescending manner in which they relate to the people they work with.

An additional question could be:

2 What sort of relationship do you think the people working with you want to have?

And

3 What are the sorts of behaviour that you might adopt which would make this relationship difficult to achieve?

When I have asked this question of groups of managers the following items emerged which could be useful for you to discuss.

Punishing mistakes One of the greatest barriers to self-development is the desire not to make a mistake. If we did not make mistakes we would never learn how to do things right. Even being told that a course of action is wrong does not stop most of us trying it out for ourselves. At times it seems the only way to learn. As a trainer and a coach, I realize that your primary objective may well be to cut out the time it takes for people to gain positive experiences, through simulating work experiences in the training room, and on the job. Managers find it frustrating watching people make the same mistakes that they did after having been told not to do it. So what has changed since childhood? It is a natural instinct. Allow people to make mistakes, provided that when they do you talk about them and they learn something. Life is about experiences, whether they are good or bad. Each has a learning point. People should be allowed to experiment, without being told:

I told you so.

Similarly, you should seek to help your managers understand the power of experience. In this way you should be able to sell them the power of practising coaching so that they experience it and not just talk about it.

Establishing trust People will produce their best for the manager and the coach they trust. You need to learn about trusting others so that they can trust you. Trust is a fragile commodity, it can take years to establish and seconds to destroy. A good friend of mine said 'Look after your name. At the end of the day it's all you've got. Tarnish it and it will take you a lifetime to shine it.'

Ask, what are the things you could do which would reduce trust in you? Some of the items I found were as follows:

- *Telling people to do something and then blaming them for the outcome if it does not work* The biggest problem with the telling style is that people will rarely do it the way you tell them. If it works, they owe the result to you. The danger is that if it does not work, then it is your fault. I also believe it is your fault.
- *Showing people up in front of others* It is difficult to bite your tongue sometimes, but the consequences of not doing so are dire. People, whether they normally get along or not, usually feel a sense of loyalty to each other when one is being attacked. The only loser in admonishing someone in public is you.
- *Talking about people behind their backs* Throw-away comments, or even planned comments, about people in front of others teaches people more about you than anything else you say. It begs the question 'What do they say about me when I'm not there?'
- *Making others aware of how much you know, or worse still, that you know something they don't* There is nothing more infuriating than being made aware by somebody in the know, that you aren't. The people we tend to trust are those who appear to know nothing. Displaying to others that you know more than them just makes them feel inferior to you, and ruins any chance that they will open up to you.

- *Failing to keep a promise* If you say you are going to do something, do it.

A couple of physical exercises that are reasonably simple to organize, and yet effective for understanding how difficult it is sometimes to trust others are as follows:

1 Put someone in the middle of a circle of colleagues. Each person's shoulders must be able to touch the shoulders of the others in the circle. When they stretch their hands out, everyone must be able to touch the person in the middle. The person in the middle must fold his arms, and close his eyes. When he is ready to fall backwards he has to say 'Ready', and let himself go. The people he falls against should push him back so that he then falls forwards. The people he falls against should in turn push him back to the middle. In reality the person in the middle will also tend to fall sideways.

After a while, ask the person in the middle what it felt like to let go. Ask the circle what it felt like having the responsibility to stop that person from falling.

2 Get someone to fold her arms, stand with her back to three colleagues, who are placed in such a way as to guarantee to stop the person from hitting the ground should she fall backwards. It is easier if one person kneels behind with arms outstretched, while one person on either side ensures that she breaks the fall into the hands of the person in the middle.

Ask the person to try it with eyes open and eyes closed.

Afterwards ask what it felt like, and what responsibility did the others feel?

3 Get someone to stand on a chair, with arms folded and his back to six colleagues standing in two lines, with arms outstretched and linked.

The questions are the same as for exercise 2. Try it facing forwards. Is there any difference?

4 Line up at least eight people, in two lines, with arms interlinked, far enough away from a volunteer who can run at the group, leap, and land as far forward as possible, into their arms. This will require the volunteer to dive into the arms of colleagues as though diving into a swimming pool.

5 Pick a person to be a tour guide, and ask the rest to leave the room. Arrange the furniture in the room in such a way that there are obstacles to climb over, but none so big that people will get hurt. The tour guide will be leading people around the room with their eyes blindfolded. Make sure you have a couple of people either side of the group to ensure that safety is maintained. The tour guide may not speak to the group, who will not be able to see, and must hold hands in a line all of the time. The tour guide may communicate with the group by sound only, but not words. It is up to the group and the guide how the code is worked out, but it cannot be explained by

using words. The task of the tour guide is to lead the group around the obstacle course by a predestined route to a target end. Bring the group in, having explained the rules.

In debrief, ask the group how confident they felt in the tour guide, what trust was established, how was it communicated? What did the guide feel?

All of us have a basic desire to trust other people, and having the trust of others placed in us gives us a sense of responsibility. Also, watching others achieve, and helping to support them is equally rewarding for the tour guide.

The discussions that ensue as a result, should reinforce the sort of characteristics and identification of possible training needs presented in the previous chapter.

The working environment is less stressful to both managers and employees

Many of the classical models of management do not seem to work. Many managers will have been exposed to Hertzberg, McGregor, Maslow, and a 1000 other gurus. In some cases, they will have returned from courses, stoked up with enthusiasm to try out the new processes of team building, management by objectives, and total quality, only to reflect a few months down the line:

Tried that—didn't work!

Creating a motivational working environment on its own sound all right, but putting it into practice for many managers is an impossibility. That fact alone produces a stressful working environment and managers.

Managers struggle to find a way to motivate people, and employees struggle to relate to managers who appear incompetent in their attempts to provide motivation. I cannot believe that the failure to translate theory into practice is a conscious thing, but merely a result of managers themselves not having a coach to help them put the theory into practice. It is rare for a manager to ask a subordinate about the training course they have just been on. Managers are *never* asked by their own manager about the course they recently attended. In this way, each teaches the other the management game. The growth of personnel functions, which find themselves dealing more and more with counselling requests as a result of employee-manager communication breakdowns, attests to the problem. All of which results in stress.

Stress is seen as a modern phenomenon resulting in such things as depression, anxiety and heart disease, and is said to be the main cause for absenteeism at work. Obviously, stress does not emanate solely from work, but it can be a major contributory factor. When people are under stress, their performance suffers. Stress is estimated to cost companies in the UK in excess of £30 billion a year. It is said that more than 20 per cent of managers will fail to reach retirement age, having suffered a heart attack, which for the greater part will have been induced by stress.

Managers can be made aware of their contribution to a stressful working environment by asking them some questions:

1 Describe the sort of behaviour that people who are suffering from stress might exhibit.

The list will probably include such items as:

- Look tired
- Off sick
- Irritable
- Slow
- Make mistakes
- Red-faced
- Disorganized
- Noticeable behaviour changes

Then ask:

2 How would you know you were suffering from stress?

The list may include some of the above items, but you are also looking for them to identify some of the following:

- Not sleeping
- Waking up early
- Not meeting the sort of deadlines that you used to be able to
- Relationship difficulties at work and at home
- Palpitations
- Headaches
- Drinking more than usual
- Day-dreaming
- Edgy

I am not saying that managers adopting the coaching principles in this book will immediately be stress-free, and that employee absenteeism will instantly be a thing of the past, simply because the company introduces a coaching programme—but it can help. There are 101 reasons why stress starts, but work performance difficulties are a major contributory factor. Employees suffering from a lack of personal performance can succumb to stress by believing that their jobs are at risk due to their poor performance. Managers with employees who are not performing suffer from stress after exhausting their attempts to motivate people whom they believe cannot be motivated. In sales teams especially, particularly in the insurance industry, managers replace employees with stunning speed, only to end up with a new set of employees who likewise under-perform. You regularly hear managers say: 'Just give me some decent people, and I'll get them to perform!'

The next question you ask could be:

3 What is it that you do as a manager, that results in the people working with you suffering from stress?

The sorts of behaviour you are looking for could include:

- Do not smile
- Shout at people
- Give them unrealistic targets and deadlines
- Give them a job to do with unclear instructions
- Do not give enough feedback and then criticize the end result
- Ignore people who are performing badly
- Ignorant of personal problems
- Unaware of inter-team rivalries or disputes
- Show favouritism

The list could be endless, and the more items the merrier.

Next ask:

4 So what could you do to reduce the potential size of this list?

The reaction you are looking for should reflect many of the items already discussed in previous chapters. The role of the manager as coach is far less stressful than the role that most managers find themselves in. This does not mean that managers abdicate their responsibility, but merely that responsibilities are equally distributed. This clear focus on performance improvement, and the desire of the manager to help employees improve their personal performance, with a structured approach available on how to do it, has stress-relieving benefits which touch both manager and employee.

The focus for many people moves from promotion to improved performance

In a large number of organizations, the focus for many staff has been unconsciously moved towards a need for individuals to increase their job grade. Many companies have become so obsessed about job evaluation, equal pay for equal value work, and job descriptions, that they have lost sight of what being at work is all about. In most major corporations, separate departments, solely concerned with the writing of job descriptions and attaching a grade to a job, have sprung up, and as a result have moved employees' main interest away from the job they do now to the job at the next grade up. Instead of people doing a job because they enjoy it, many employees are now seeking roles further up the grade ladder, no matter what it involves, and no matter what their personal level of ability is. Indeed someone once said to me:

The greater the level of incompetence individuals have, the greater their belief that they are competent to do the next job up.

I am not saying that coaching will rid companies of this nonsense, but it will detract the attention of individuals away from this almost paranoic desire to move up the ladder, towards improving their performance in the current job. Having said that, I accept that for the employee, promotion may represent performance improvement, and may also be seen as a reward for good performance. The point is worthy of discussion in terms of establishing what it is the employee really wants. As I have said before, many people at work derive little satisfaction from roles that are unfulfilling. It could be that by introducing a coaching ethos in which people are encouraged to reach performance goals previously unconsidered, promotion may not after all be the end reward. Whatever the outcome, the chances are that decisions about job enhancement or promotion will be made for the right reasons. If a coaching ethos also in some way influences the demise of what I see as a totally non-productive expense of the 1980s and 1990s, then so much the better.

Specific examples of these benefits at work are contained in Chapter 8, 'The coach in action'.

Summary

- Even though managers are able to define the descriptions of good managers and bad managers, many will admit to displaying the behaviours of bad managers a lot of the time. Putting theory into practice is harder than it sounds.
- Managers often cite 'lack of time' as the main reason for not coaching staff, and yet effective managers have as much time as non-effective managers. The former utilize their time better.
- The major benefits of coaching are that people perform the job better, the relationship between the manager and the subordinate is enhanced, the working environment is less stressful, and the focus for many people moves from promotion to improved job performance.
- Many workers achieve more in their private lives than they do at work.
- The differences between what managers believe motivates employees to increased job performance and what workers themselves believe can be substantial. Managers still believe that people are mainly motivated by reward, whereas large numbers of people still seek self-fulfilment and job satisfaction.
- The behaviours that managers adopt which lead people to dislike them are punishing mistakes and failing to establish trust.
- The sort of things managers do which reduce trust are telling people to do something and then blaming them if it goes wrong; showing people up in front of others.

Recommended reading

Bailey, Roy (1989) *50 Activities for Managing Stress*. Gower.

Belbin, R. Meredith (1981) *Management Teams: Why they Succeed or Fail*. Butterworth Heinemann.

Choppin, John (1991) *Quality Through People: A Blueprint for Proactive Total Quality Management*. IFS Publications.

Clutterbuck, David and Crainer, Stuart (1990) *Makers of Management, Men and Women Who Changed the Business World*. Guild Publishing.

Dowling, William F. and Sayles, Leonard R. (1978) *How Managers Motivate*. McGraw-Hill, 2nd edn.

Kennedy, Carol (1991) *Guide to the Management Gurus*. Random Century.

Kiechel, Walter (1985) 'The managerial midlife crisis', *Fortune*, 11 November.

Leavitt, Harold J., Pondy, Louis R. and Boje, David M. (eds) (1989) *Readings in Managerial Psychology*. University of Chicago Press, 4th edn.

Margerison, Charles J. (1991) 'Do you work under pressure?', *Training and Management Development Methods*, Vol. 5. MCB University Press.

Steers, Richard M. and Porter, Lyman W. (1987) *Motivation and Work Behaviour.* McGraw-Hill, 4th edn.

Stuart, Roger (1991) 'Characterising stress', Parts 1 and 2, *Journal of European Industrial Training,* **15** (2)(3).

4 Where do you start?

This chapter introduces a system of training needs analysis known as whole–part–whole. It shows managers how to identify the specific area of coaching focus. Is job success a matter of knowledge or skill application, and where does attitude fit in? The effect of focusing on the negative is discussed. Also covered is the importance of practice, and the inevitable drop in performance that should be expected during skill acquisition.

Knowledge, skills and attitudes

The first thing you need to achieve with managers is to decide what the main elements of the job being coached are.

Ask your managers to determine the elements that make up a total job performance in the three areas of basic knowledge, skills and attitude. Take each separately, and ask managers to rate the importance of each on a scale of 4, where 4 = essential, 3 = very important, 2 = important and 1 = desirable. It should be relatively easy to reach consensus on knowledge, although some managers will include skill items. However long it takes, make certain that those items remaining on the list are knowledge—that which the individual has to know to do the job. It is also worth questioning some of the knowledge assumptions that managers have about the job. Your task should be to question what is meant by 'basic knowledge', something which usually comes up. How in-depth should employees' knowledge be to do the job, or should they simply know where to look for that knowledge?

When I left school I began work in the Magistrates' Courts as an Assistant to the Clerk to the Justices. Although a fancy title, I quickly found myself making tea and filling ink-wells. It was not long before talent was spotted and I rose within two years to answering the telephone. I eventually left when I realized that either I had to get a new brain or I would have to wait until my twentieth employment anniversary before I could pass the kettle on to someone else. I recall the younger clerks (in their thirties), when they needed to know something always sought out the Deputy Clerk to the Justices. He was also young to be in the job compared to most of his peer group, but rather than seek out the older Justices' Clerks, who invariably told them and us lesser mortals the answer immediately, he had the habit of not telling us. He showed us where to look, and in this way we learnt more by finding out for ourselves. He was probably the first coach I met.

In many organizations more time is spent drumming knowledge into people rather than skills—to what end? If your product is dynamic and keeps changing, then knowledge has a short shelf-life, whereas skill can always be on the increase. If as much time and resource was spent on skills acquisition as is spent on knowledge accumulation, performance levels could shoot through the roof. Each job will be uniquely different, however, it will be interesting to note the usual disagreement that ensues with regard to the coaching starting point—knowledge.

The next area gets even more interesting. Let us suppose that the job you and the managers are looking at involves a series of communication skills such as:

- Questioning
- Listening
- Presenting

Is listening a skill or an attitude? It is a worthy debate. Do people have poor listening skills because of a lack of training, or a lack of interest? Is listening a matter of poor attitude, or poor hearing? Are people bad at asking questions because they do not know how, or they lack the motivation to find out about other people? Is the manner in which people communicate a matter of training, or of conditioning, and if the latter, is that attitude? What is skill? Is it an innate ability that you are born with? Can anybody acquire any sort of skill? If it is attitude, can you change attitude?

Most things are to do with attitude. It is certain that we can all, barring physical disability, already perform most of the skills that we are being asked to perform at work. That is to say, we can physically perform those skills, given time, practice and feedback. So what stops us? What stops people performing the skills we expect of them at work, to the level we want? Ask your managers the same question:

What stops your people performing these skills at the level you want?

Usually managers will come up with a list which resembles the following:

- Wrong person for the job
- Bad attitude
- Not motivated
- Useless
- I did not pick them

A classic is the latter, known as the 'inheritance factor'. Many managers will deliberately focus on the people they did not employ and who are under-performing, and happily forget those they picked who are under-performing. A basic premiss of the coaching philosophy is that everyone has the skill to do the job you are asking them to do. The answer lies in how to extract that performance and to accept management responsibility for the task.

Once your managers have determined the knowledge, skills and attitudes required to do the job, you need to ask them to identify those

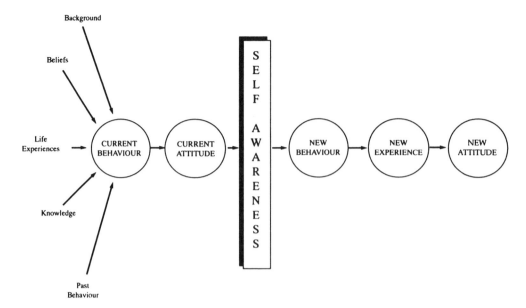

Figure 4.1   *Changing attitudes*

items across all three areas which are critical to success. In the main, they should by now be picking attitudes, although in some cases there will be areas of knowledge and skill which may also be critical, unless they have been moved into the attitude list.

So if it is attitude, what can you do about it? Some people will say that you cannot change attitude, but I believe you can. People are not born with an attitude, they acquire one through beliefs and feelings and experiences throughout their lives, and in this way attitude can be a dynamic entity. As we get older, however, we take on board fewer attitude-changing beliefs, as we harden ourselves to the pain of change. Attitude can best be described by referring to Figure 4.1. Our background, our life experiences, the past behaviours we see and adopt, together with the knowledge and beliefs we collect determine our current behaviour and hence our current attitude. Our attitude will be changed by an increasing self-awareness which produces a new behaviour, leads to new experiences and develops into a new attitude. The coach, by helping the performer become more aware, by encouraging new behaviours, can also assist the individual to gain the sort of attitude that winners need.

Behaviour

An easy way to show how attitudes change is to ask delegates at the beginning of a course to write down their thoughts about their colleagues on the course before they get to know each other. Obviously this depends on how well the group already knows each other, and yet even in those gatherings where supposedly they know each other, it can be surprising how little they do know. At the end of the event ask all delegates to go through the list again and note any changes in opinions they now have. Most will have changed their initial opinions or modified them in some way. What is opinion but a component of attitude? Our attitudes are changed about each other simply by being together for a period of time. It is a good lesson for coaches to learn also. The more time people spend together, the more they get to like each other. Like so many 'wives's tales', 'familiarity' does not breed contempt, but liking. In many organizations suffering from the 'them and us' syndrome, the easiest thing to do is to get managers and employees to spend more time together—which is just what coaching as a philosophy does.

The next stage is to determine what it is that individuals do that displays a certain attitude, or skill, or knowledge. What is it that an individual *does*, behaviourally, that leads you to believe that he or she has a certain attitude, level of skill or knowledge? If you can identify specifically what it is that someone does, you can set about, with him or her making the necessary changes in order to improve performance levels.

Determining successful and unsuccessful behaviour

The way to determine which are successful and which are unsuccessful behaviours is to examine in detail the performance of both effective and non-effective employees and to isolate the different behaviours, that is the behaviours which make the difference (Figure 4.2, page 46).

Ask your managers to do the following:

Think of three individuals in your team, two who are performing well, and one who is performing not so well. Write their names down. Let us call the two who are doing well A and B, and the one who is not performing well C. What do A and B do, that C does not?

Make sure that they express actual behaviours, and not assumptions or characteristics or personality traits. That is why managers have to visualize the three people they are thinking of. It helps to write their names down. This exercise in itself will highlight the need for a systematic approach to the development of individuals. Managers can hardly change the behaviour of their staff if they do not have a record of that behaviour, and the only way to collect this information is by observation. It is no good talking about empowering employees when the manager is totally oblivious to what it is the individual is capable of. Many managers compile this information in discussions with employees, which is better than no discussion at all. Those managers who have difficulty with this session of writing down behaviours will be those managers who rarely observe people at their work. Observing and guiding people to performance improvement is *the* reason for management. It is the starting point of determining current performance, identifying the next positive step to take and empowering employees to deliver of their personal best (Figure 4.3, page 47).

This process of listing behaviours should produce an inventory of positive factors derived from what A and B do, which will in turn provide ample discussion points between different managers. Do not be too con-

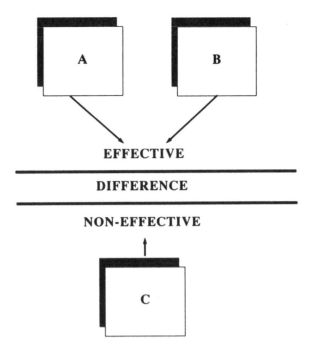

Figure 4.2   *The difference between effective and non-effective behaviours*

cerned that different managers or groups of managers appear to disagree. The discussion that you should encourage after identifying the positive factors will most likely resolve some of those issues, and in any event, the premiss of good coaching is that people tend to do the job differently anyway. With luck, you will end up with a consensus of opinion of the positive factors that enhance job performance. Do the exercise again, once more focusing on two good performers and one poor performer.

Carry on this process until the managers can no longer identify sufficient numbers to make up threes.

These then are the positive factors that enhance job performance for your managers. It is a crude method, but it will give your managers something to work with in the field, and should also allow you to draw up a profile for the ideal behaviours that you want the people you are coaching to display. Before we go on to that, what about the negative factors?

You simply repeat the above process in reverse. Picking two people who are under-performing and one who is performing well, and carrying out the same process as above, will produce a set of negative factors.

What you and your managers will now have is a set of behaviours that you want to encourage, and a set of behaviours that you want to discourage. These, therefore, are the elements that you want to work with, and which your managers will focus on in the field, or at the workplace with the people they are coaching. But remember to tackle all of the

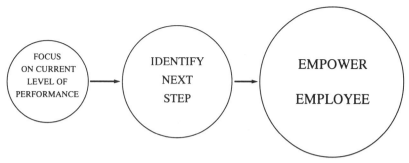

Figure 4.3 *Observing and guiding*

items identified at once is impossible, and the reason why many managers are ineffective trainers is that, faced with perceived time pressures, they try to do too much at once. Rome was not built in a day and neither was sustained performance improvement.

Whole–part–whole

Many people new to coaching, and even those with years of experience in training, make the mistake of trying to do too much all in one go. On field visits, managers try and improve a person's total performance, bombarding the employee with so much information, whether confirmed in detail in writing or not, which depresses and confuses those being coached. Managers believe that their time is valuable, and therefore they have to utilize the time spent with an individual to the fullest extent. They fail to realize that it is not the time spent that counts but the quality of that time. Likewise it is not the manager's agenda that is important, it is what the individual wants that is more relevant, and eventually what will work. Let us imagine that we are describing the job of a trainer. What positive behaviours may have been identified for the job? The list could include:

- Plans time effectively
- Actively seeks opinions of managers
- Dresses smartly
- Rehearses presentation
- Uses presentation aids
- Adopts a positive approach

The list could be longer, shorter, or totally different—it matters not. For you it represents the total effective performance of a trainer (Figure 4.4, page 48). Usually, someone training the trainer first observes the trainer carrying out the job role, he or she observes the full performance, and then tries to put the full performance right. The same goes for any job normally being observed. In order for the method of coaching recommended by the POWER model to work, both coach and person being coached should agree that while the coach will watch the full performance, he or she will only concentrate on one area for the coaching session. Let us assume in this instance that both have agreed to look at how the individual uses presentation aids. Between them, they should

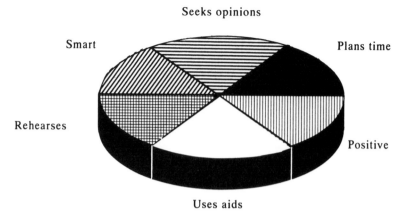

Figure 4.4 *Trainer attributes*

agree what the component parts of this area of performance are, and collate a further 'whole' performance list (Figure 4.5). For our purposes, 'using presentation aids' could involve the following:

- The use of an overhead projector.
- The presenter is clean and works effectively.
- The overhead slides are clear and uncluttered.
- The presentation medium is able to be used interactively.
- The presentation visuals are shown and explained.

This then represents the whole performance that the manager will observe, and from this observation, the manager will attempt to elicit from his or her subordinate which parts of that specific area of the performance the subordinate believes could have been improved.

By improving one area of the performance it will expand the skill, and then by replacing it into the total performance, it will in turn expand and improve total performance (Figure 4.6). This process, used repeatedly, improving small areas of performance and replacing them into the whole performance, will bring about a far more lasting and effective increase in performance than any usual training session.

Obviously, the exercise just described, of breaking down total performance areas into manageable size chunks is something that you can focus on in workshops with your managers. The better prepared they are when they see their staff, the more effective they will be in the workplace. It will be important for you to insist, however, that the identification of the specific area of focus of coaching for the day is ideally left to the individual being coached. The coach should only suggest the area of focus if the individual cannot come up with an item that he or she wants to improve. If that happens, then it also says a lot about the attitude of that person and perhaps the day would be better spent focusing on his or her attitude rather than actual job performance. Those people who appear not to have any development needs, are usually those who are performing at a fraction of their potential.

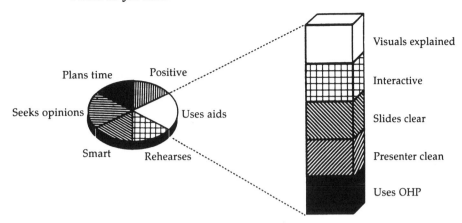

Figure 4.5 *Development of trainer attributes*

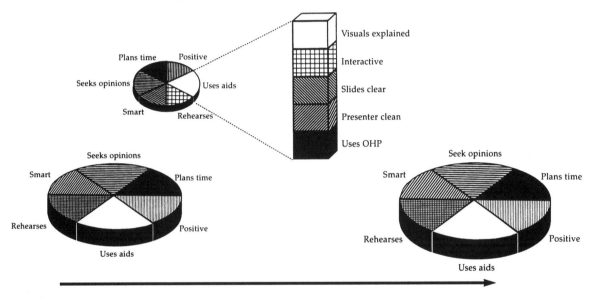

Figure 4.6 *Improving part, improves the whole*

Focusing on negative performance

If your managers have people who are consistently performing very badly, and they fit into and exceed the negative behaviours you have identified in job performance, then the coaching session can follow the 'whole–part–whole' system, but can also be more directive.

The chances are that these people will not come up with an item they want to improve in, other than, in the example used of coaching a trainer:

If I had a proper overhead projector my presentations would be better.

They can usually be those people that the manager finds most difficult to change. In fact there are two categories that managers usually have problems with:

- Those performing at a very high level.
- Those performing at a very low level.

The first category is more problematic, and is dealt with in Chapter 8, 'The coach in action'. The latter requires less subtlety. For example:

MANAGER   'In my experience, those performing below the standards we have in our team, usually display one or all of these behaviours—in which area would you say you need improvement?'

Failure by the individual to identify an item leaves you with little choice but to tell him or her, and more than that:

MANAGER   'It is of great concern to me that you consistently under-perform, but more than that. You fail to understand why you under-perform, other than it is probably someone else's fault. My purpose today is to: help you establish some personal responsibility for your performance; identify what you are specifically going to focus on to improve your performance; and set a deadline for that improvement. Alternatively, you may decide that you would be more comfortable in a team with lower standards, and lower personal expectations.'

You see, unless people accept personal responsibility for their performance, then coaching will not work. It is probably the main reason why coaching does not work for many people. The problem is not that the coaching is ineffective, but the individual has not accepted responsibility for personal performance.

The other part about negativity is the manager who focuses constantly on the negative and brings about exactly the behaviour he or she is trying to eradicate. Many managers come from the management by exception school of management, in which managers focus only on those things that are going wrong. It gives them a jaundiced view of people. They are only ever presented with problems to solve, and therefore believe that without them the organization would not continue. If all you get all day long is bad news, then you will begin to believe that only bad news exists. If the only time the manager contacts a subordinate is when he or she has done something wrong, then the subordinate in turn will associate the manager with things that go wrong. In this sort of environment, the coach/person being coached relationship never even gets off the ground.

It is however understandable. As parents we tend to tell our children *not* to do something negative rather than to do something positive. How many of you have said:

Don't stay out late.

And sat worrying about them as they missed the last bus home?

Try this:

Fill a glass to the brim with water and ask someone to walk across the room to you after instructing him or her—'Whatever you do, don't spill the water.' If it looks like he or she might manage it, keep saying 'Don't spill the water.' Inevitably it will be spilt. Pick someone else and instruct him or her thus—'I want you to bring the full glass of water to me, carrying the glass in a straight line, and look at me when you are walking.' Chances are he or she will arrive with the glass of water intact.

Personal responsibility

I have already said that managers cannot be held responsible for the personal performance of others, only for their own, but that in itself does not tell the whole story. While managers cannot be held responsible for the personal performance of others, that does not stop them being responsible for attempting to make individuals aware of their personal responsibility. Part of the job of the manager in coaching sessions with their staff, is to help employees accept and understand whose ultimate responsibility it is to improve performance. Having achieved that, and that in itself is no mean task, the other thing is that the action to improve performance has to be immediate. The point of personal responsibility and of personal improvement goals is that you can be better at a particular skill today than you were yesterday. What is important here is the word 'today'. Most goals are set for tomorrow:

I'll start that diet tomorrow. As soon as I get the time.... After I come back from holiday.... When I've finished this packet of cigarettes....

Personal effectiveness and responsibility for performance improvement only really happen when dealt within the immediate time-scale.

In order to acquire a skill, to improve a skill, or to retain a skill, there has to be desire, commitment and determination from the individual. The coach, however, can be the catalyst. Being the best is a very laudable goal, but then the only performance that can be controlled is your own. You may be the best you can be, but on the day someone else may be better. The most a coach and an individual can expect is to be the best they have it within them to be. In this process the coach has a significant role to play.

The starting point in skills acquisition is to realize that we all begin with a certain level of skills. We are all performing at our current level of innate skill. The skills we have acquired throughout our lifetime journey so far, have been learnt, practised and become innate. In other words, we start not being able to do something through a lack of a skill, or because the skill is not polished and therefore clumsy in execution; through persistence, practice and repetition the skill is then learnt until we are able to carry out a particular task without thinking about it. For example, in Figure 4.7 (page 52), on the bottom left-hand of the scale is what I call an innate inability—not being able to do something is either innate, or has become innate through non-usage. Even at that level though, there are some skills which are innate, and we have certain abilities already. Babies do not need training to seek food. They will move their heads and mouths and seek food. These are the internal 'motor' skills. They are to do with the way in which we can already, without training, do certain physical things. That is why when some people say:

I can't do that

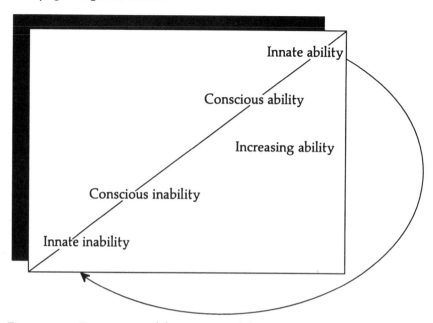

Figure 4.7 *From innate inability to innate ability*

I would say that they choose not to. Sometimes through telling ourselves that we cannot do something, we appear to lose the skill to be
able to do something. We create an innate inability—we coach ourselves not to be able to do something.

It is easy enough to relate much of this to athletic processes, but how
does this apply to the use of skills at work, if our work does not involve
athleticism? I believe that most processes at work do involve athleticism,
of a different, and yet a very similar kind. For example, let us look at
the job of a counsellor. The most successful counsellors, in terms of
helping a client to accept a problem and solve it, are most usually also
the most skilled at communication. They are the people who have the
ability to bring about an end result over and over again, which is
brought about by the performance they deliver. In this case the end
result may just be the client accepting the change of circumstances. The
same could be said of a VDU operator, where the task may be simple,
but the absence of errors could be critical. The skills being used may be
repetitive, but the concentration needed crucial. Each person, however,
even in jobs which are the same, delivers a unique performance. In the
delivery of that unique performance, people use a series of skills, physical
and emotional, which through continuous practice and employment
produce consistently high performance ends. While at the outset many
of those skills will have been awkward, over a period of time they will
have become innate. If you are a driver, think back to when you were
learning. You probably made a number of mistakes. Many of them at
the time may have affected your confidence, and what looked an easy
task when watching someone else carry it out, became less certain as
you realized that it was not as easy as you thought. Over a period of

time, however, you learnt to drive, and after a while much of the process of driving became automatic. Like many drivers you will also have been on a journey, especially on a motorway, and suddenly realized that you had passed a number of junctions, but could not remember the journey. So if you were not concentrating, how did you manage to drive the car? The skill had become innate. The process of driving safely, keeping the speed down, checking your mirror, slowing and speeding up when necessary has for most of us become an innate function. We do not have to think about it any more. There are advantages and disadvantages to this. One advantage is that we do not have to clutter our brains thinking about things which can be done automatically. The main disadvantage is that the performance of a particular task becomes so comfortable, that most of us then settle for the easy life, maintain the performance level we have achieved and then never move forward.

An easy exercise to do with your managers when explaining this is to throw a sponge ball at one of the group without warning, and then to as many of the others as it takes the drive the point home. Most will catch it, and yet it is not something we are born being consciously able to do. Having learnt how, however, most of us will retain the skill. Then ask a member of the group to juggle two balls. You have to be really unlucky to pick someone who can, but even then it will become a learning point. The question is:

Why can you not juggle two balls, and yet clearly a juggler can?

Easy—the juggler has practised. But more than that. Some jugglers will be able to juggle three, four and more. The way they build up to that, however, is first to throw and catch one, then two, then three, and then by stages up to the number they can physically manage. At each stage they will wait until the ability becomes innate.

I have observed hundreds of people performing their jobs, where it is possible to see how those with the desire to improve their physical delivery have in time improved the outcome of their job. Likewise, I have seen those with emotional barriers such as:

I've always done it this way. I can't do that. I can't say that.

As a consequence, these people continue to deliver a poor performance and deliver less than acceptable results.

Does that mean that you have to aim for perfection? Certainly not, unless you define perfection as trying to be the best you can be. Perfection, by my definition, is not attainable. That is not to say that some people fool themselves into believing that they have achieved it. Whether they admit it or not is another matter. There are those people who ease into a comfortable performance—they stay in their comfort zone, and in performance terms, stand still. That standing still, and delivering the same performance, may be acceptable. It may be higher than others. In fact the 'standing still syndrome' is quite usual in top performers. For many people, performing at a level above colleagues is what it is all about:

So long as I can keep a step ahead, that's all I want.

Paradoxically, I found the people performing at a high level also have great feelings of insecurity. Being out in front is just as stressful as being way behind. In many ways, being out in front can be more stressful. There is in their minds only one way to go—down. At least the person at the bottom, having hit bottom, can say that the only way now is up. In a lot of ways, coaches have more difficulty getting top performers to increase their skills, ability and performance, than they have with low performers, and yet the same process and rules apply.

External and genetic factors apart, we should all begin with the same opportunity to display a certain level of skill. Clearly, however, our physical make-up also determines our physical abilities. It is hard to imagine that if you are 5 ft 2 in tall, that you would survive in a basketball team. If you have short stubby fingers, then you could struggle to play classical guitar. But then, how does physical make-up affect a skills-based performance at work? I suggest that the vast majority of people at work play on the same level pitch physically. That is not denying that some are more attractive than others, and evidence does exist to show that 'attractiveness' helps in getting your message across. So does that mean, if your looks are less than perfect, that successful performance is a pipe-dream? Obviously not. In many ways, those that believe that they have a head start, either through real or perceived physical advantage, sometimes lack the drive to apply themselves.

The delivery of a performance, therefore, depends not just on your physical make-up, but on what you do about it. That leads me to believe that the emotional processes involved in skills acquisition are of greater importance than the existence of a physical capability.

Pivotal to my belief in the potential of individuals is the conviction that we all choose the level of performance we wish to deliver. Whether that performance is at work or play it is a choice that we will at some stage make consciously. The coach's job is to expose current performance to the coached person's conscious mind.

To move from innate inability to conscious inability is for many people a momentous step. It requires people to accept that their current level of performance is their personal responsibility. That they choose to deliver at that level. Those performing at a low level (innate inability) will most usually refuse to accept this proposition. Those performing at a high level (innate ability) take it too much for granted, and stand still. In order to move the latter group forward, the coach has to help the individual accept that he or she has to go through the loop again. Those who do, become champions—that is why there are so few of them. Most choose not to.

The biggest step then is the first one. In order to move forward, each person has to accept and understand that he or she alone is responsible for current performance levels. Sometimes that can be uncomfortable to deal with, and unfortunately, left to their own devices, many will choose not to deal with it. This, coupled with my comments about each person being an individual, makes coaching a problem for many organizations. It only works on a one-to-one basis. There are few parts of the process that can work in groups. The theory can be explained to a group. Support systems can be set up among groups. Dependent upon the size, self-disclosure can be done in groups. Total self-awareness, however, is a private thing. It is doubtful whether people reach a state of self-awareness with any other person present at all. Whatever the reality of that, coaches can only operate, and be effective on a one-to-one basis. That is why true coaching is greatly misunderstood. Organizations are trying to *coach* groups, when what they mean is *training*. You can train a group of people, you cannot coach them. You coach individuals.

The dynamics of groups are complicated and can result in unexpected outcomes. There is no guarantee that many of the methods I have outlined will produce anything but adverse results when tried in groups, or vice versa. In particular, if the coach has to be directive, coaxing the individual to repeat a poor performance until it improves, the group could support the individual either to improve or to resist what it may see as persecution. It is best to steer away from the problems.

Stage one, therefore, is in self-awareness of the responsibility for current performance. How long could that take? It will vary from individual to individual, and from activity to activity, together with the potential complexity of the skill.

Part of the problem associated with skills acquisition is the varying rate of progress. At the beginning of the learning process, progress can be enhanced by the enthusiasm and determination of the person being coached. Gradually the rate of progression is likely to slow down, which can be discouraging. The individual can reach a plateau (Figure 4.8, page 56). Many never leave it. There is an assumption anyway that a level is reached beyond which improvement is impossible. Not that long ago, it was assumed that man could not travel faster that ten miles an hour before losing consciousness. Like the great athletes, we have to get used to the idea that every record can be broken. The coach's job is to give encouragement in the face of adversity, whether it be plateauing or an actual setback. People have to believe that what they are attempting is possible, even if no one else has ever achieved it. This is a classic example of why the coach does not need to have achieved the very thing being attempted by the person being coached. It is not necessary for the sales coach to have been a top selling salesperson. Sales success is no guarantee for sales management success, or sales training success. To be a great piano teacher, you need not have been a great concert pianist. To be a great art teacher, you do not have to be a Picasso.

Of far greater importance is the ability to recognize when people need encouragement, when they need direction and when they need help. Coaches sometimes can instruct people, when it is appropriate. The skill is in knowing when.

Developing managers as coaches

Performance
level

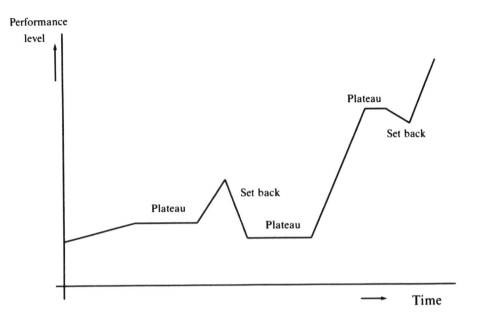

Figure 4.8 *A pattern of skill acquisition*

Coaches help people to realize that when a plateau of performance is reached, that this is normal. It is also quite normal to have setbacks. The measure of top performers, however, is what they do in the face of setbacks. We are all reasonably good at dealing with situations when things are going well. We do not tend to react too well when things are not going so well. The skill of the coach is to understand how unsettling it is for the performer and to give support. Most people, when faced with adversity, or even minor challenges, believe they are unique in their failure. It can be very reassuring to find that most people have remarkably similar feelings of doubt.

A further phenomenon to be aware of is the entering of the 'danger and opportunity zone' (Figure 4.9). I have found, that for the vast majority of people, when learning a new skill, overall performance can drop, sometimes dramatically. It can fall to an interim level, while the skill is being practised. It is partially the danger zone because this is where trainees want to give up, going back to their old level of performance, and trainers or managers let them. It is also the opportunity zone because a potential level of performance, much higher than their current level, beckons not far away. What is needed however, is an understanding that performance can drop initially, and that it is not unusual or an indicator of potential failure, but an indicator of potential success.

Think about a footballer learning a new free kick. For a while he will look as though he lacks skill, missing the target with regularity. The problem is that no one sees the failure, fans only witness the end result, on the football pitch. Most people at a race meeting will not stand at the

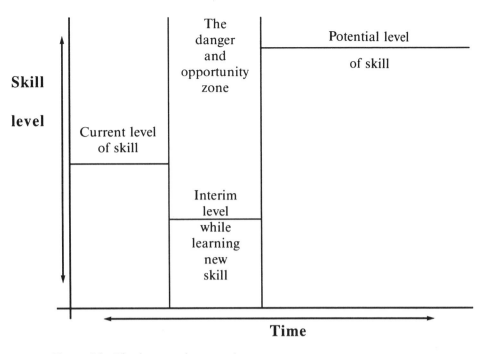

Figure 4.9 The danger and opportunity zone

starting line, they are only interested in the finish, and yet most athletes know that how you start is probably more important than how you finish. People pay a considerable amount of money to see the likes of Eric Clapton, or Luciano Pavarotti produce their best performance at a concert, without much thought to the practice that will have gone before. That practice will have sounded for a part of the time as though amateurs were at play, whereas a poor performance in practice can be the mark of a true professional. Great actors will not walk on stage and deliver a series of lines after a first reading. It takes them time to learn the words, after which they concentrate on their performance. The same rules apply to all jobs which have a skill element. During practice, performance will fall. It is far better that decline in performance is seen on the practice pitch rather than at the cup final. It has been my experience that most people try practising in live performances, when it matters most to get it right. The experience of failing in a live performance dents their confidence, which in turn makes them return to their old performance habits. This rationale, more than any other, is the reason why many people fail to realize their true performance potential. A classic retort is:

It's no good, when I tried that once before it didn't work!

Most will have tried it no more than once. The presence of the coach during those practice sessions is of vital importance. If both coach and individual are committed to improving performance, it is at this stage that the coach can become extremely directive, sometimes forcing the individual to repeat the performance again and again until he or she gets it right. There is nothing wrong with the coach slipping into pure training mode when it is appropriate.

Some coaches will demonstrate the skill, which while laudable in one sense is dangerous in another. The coach's performance may not give a clear indication of the skill necessary. In the same way that showing films or videos of experts performing the skill is of doubtful value. If used at all they should be brief, and preferably cover a specific point or area which the people being coached are experiencing difficulty in executing. They can be useful for giving an example of the type and variety of performances and also to reinforce when someone says:

I can't do that

Or

That's impossible.

It can prove that it can be done, or that it is possible. That is not to say, however, that the make-up of the individual matches exactly that of the performance being shown. Each person is an individual and each must find his or her own way of delivering a unique performance. The best way for each person to learn is to:

Just do it!

In my view the coach should be facilitating the skill. This can be enhanced by the performers watching themselves on video rather than someone else. It is of far greater value to individuals to have themselves recorded, and to see their performance with a coach present, than to watch someone else's performance. Most people neither hear themselves nor see themselves perform their skills. I found over a five-year period that 99 per cent of salespeople, whose job entailed telephoning clients for appointments, had never recorded themselves or had their voices recorded for them so that they could hear how they actually sounded. The vast majority of British managers have had no communication training, and of those that have, a tiny minority have actually seen and heard themselves in role play. Most people, whose jobs involve the spoken word, and face-to-face relationships with others at work, have no idea what they sound like or look like in action. It is not so much a case of 'In the land of the blind the one-eyed man is King' as 'There are none so blind as will not see, and none so deaf as will not hear.'

People make a great assumption about how they sound and how they look. Looking in the mirror in the morning is exactly that—a mirror image. It is about as useful for self-awareness as looking at an old photograph of yourself in the morning. In fact I contend that huge numbers of people see an image of themselves which is rarely based on reality, but on an old photograph of how they used to be, or even an ideal drawing of how they want to be. The very first thing people say when seeing themselves for the first time on video is:

I look terrible.

Yet people look at themselves in the mirror at least once every day and do not say the same thing as when they see themselves on video. The problem is, we see what we want to see. The same thing happens with voice development. The only way to get people to understand how to develop their voice is to let them hear it. The voice people hear in their heads is not the voice everyone else hears. Dependent on how thick people's skulls are, the voice heard by the individual inside the head is naturally dulled to some extent. It has a different resonance to the way others hear it. As with video, people mostly say when hearing their voice played back:

That's not me.

Well who is it? People have to be faced with reality, depressing or not.

Recording and playing back on video should not just be restricted to salespeople or managers. There are hundreds of jobs which would benefit from being recorded and played back to the individual. Most people I accept are self-conscious when being recorded, but if you leave the video switched on for a while and walk away, most people will eventually relax. The thing to remember about playing it back, however, is only to do so on a one-to-one basis. Nothing is more boring than watching other people on video.

Telling and expectations

I have discussed how people already have a substantial amount of information in terms of basic knowledge of the task and the skill expected of them in performing that task. For this reason, telling people what to do, in most cases, produces an adverse reaction. I accept that having knowledge of the task and skill does not necessarily guarantee that the individual will perform that task either properly or effectively. What I submit, however, is that most people know what is expected of them.

That is not to say that they consciously know where they currently are in relation to what is expected. The coach's job is to bring that reality into the individual's conscious state. People are very good at procrastinating. They are adept at placing at the back of their minds, tasks and chores which need accomplishing. Moreover, it is no good the coach simply asking people where they believe they are, in terms of a skill level, and leaving it at that.

While the coach can and often does direct, direction should be used sparingly, and any instructions given need to be simple. I found that the more instructions that are given, and especially if they are complicated, the higher the risk of possible rejection by the trainee, and failure usually follows. In this scenario, the person being coached will tend to blame his or her coach, and the trainer/manager will blame the trainee/subordinate for a poor performance effort. The point about complicated instructions is that the human brain can only hold one thought in the conscious mind at a time. While the subconscious is capable of holding millions of pieces of information, our conscious brain can only deal with them one at a time.

For example, in coaching a new skill, or improving an old one, what you are doing is asking the individual to bring the required new actions into the conscious mind in order to deal with them. Have you ever seen parents trying to teach children how to swim? You should listen to the multitude of instructions they give, and then watch what happens when they let go. They sink:

Lift your head up, and kick your feet, and try and keep your bottom up, just go for the other side, and pull your arms back after you've made a 'v' shape.

It is a wonder anybody learns how to swim at all. What happens in reality is that we eventually switch off from all of the instructions and 'have a go'. The feelings we experience from staying afloat teach us more than 1000 well meant directions.

The subconscious is a very powerful tool. It runs the machine when we are not paying attention. If you drive a car, your subconscious probably does more driving than your conscious. You learnt the processes one at a time, but when it comes to driving, you have to produce a lot of them together. Think about turning a corner. You have to ease off the accelerator, indicate, brake, check the mirror, turn the wheel, and yet the chances are that not a great deal of thought goes into it. You just sort of do it. The things you tend to think about are making the tea, getting to your appointment, the person you are going to meet, music or a discussion on the radio.

Most of us go through the same learning process. Too many instructions at once confuse us, and we fail. One at a time and we can cope. Skills coaching is about taking the skills one at a time, dealing with it, and helping the individual to put that skill into the subconscious so that in effect it becomes innate. It can then be performed naturally, but not necessarily effectively. Driving a car, for a lot of people, has therefore become an innate skill, though not in many cases perfect—even though the vast majority of people might think it is, and that is a major problem for the coach. Many people believe that they are all right as they are:

I'm getting along just fine, things might not be spectacular, but they are all right.

The coach has to encourage individuals to open their minds, and the way to do that is to ask the sort of questions in Chapter 6. The key to good guidance and instruction lies in what the coach says, and just as importantly in how it is said. The movement from innate inability to the stages of conscious inability and to conscious ability are difficult for many people. At one end of the spectrum you are highlighting people who are self-conscious about their failings, and at the other exposing people to awkward delivery of a skill, something that sometimes they believe they will never master. It depends on how the coach encourages and feeds back to the performers. Granted some people need to be pushed, but most want to be encouraged.

Let us go back to the dartboard. Set up your two teams again. The task is to hit the Bull's Eye. Brief one manager that each time a team member misses the target he has to ridicule him, and then ask the next person to throw. In the other team the manager encourages anyone who misses to throw again, highlighting when they get closer, asking what they could do differently if they get worse, and really congratulating when they hit the target. Record both sessions separately. I guarantee that in the latter team, more people will hit the target more often than in the first team— why? We need encouragement to try again in order to succeed. If you end on a failure, you will remember the failure, and when it comes to performing the task again, you expect to fail. It becomes the self-fulfilling prophesy.

The expectation of the coach that the individual can and will win is a powerful tool. Most successful managers I know believe that their people can and will win. This is not false expectation but the knowledge that confidence brings—confidence in their ability and in the ability of their people. A very successful regional sales director in a major sales force recently said to me:

My region runs on expectations. I expect to win, and the team knows what is expected of them.

This knowledge of management expectations is important. In too many companies the company vision and expectations of success never get past senior management, while most of the troops do not know what is expected of them. It would be like being the captain of ship where you know where you are going, but you forgot to tell the man at the helm. How many helmsmen are there aimlessly wandering around in your company?

Ask your managers to write down the individual names of the people in their work teams on the form in Appendix 1. In the right-hand column ask them to rate their people on a scale of 1 to 10, where 10 is high and 1 is low. When they have done this, ask them to isolate the people who scored less than 7. Then ask:

What will happen to these people?

The chances are that these people will either end up leaving, or will be dismisssed because of unacceptable performance. The next thing on which to generate discussion is:

If you have therefore already made up your mind about these people, how does that fit into the coaching philosophy?

The next stage is to ask the managers to describe in detail how they believe they treat the two sets of people, using the form in Appendix 2. You may want to spice up the discussion by saying that you have already canvassed the individuals in the team to ask them what their perceptions of equal treatment are!

Perhaps a more direct question about their own feelings would be more pertinent:

Think of a manager who is more successful than you—I know it is difficult— and then write down the behaviours you believe your boss adopts with that person that are different to the way that your boss behaves with you.

Every encounter between a manager and a subordinate involves learning of some kind. I have often told managers that people learn more in one hour with a manager than they do in a month with a trainer. The attitudes, habits and expectations of workers themselves will be reinforced or modified to some degree as a result of every meeting with the manager, whether they operate as coach or not. The day-to-day experience of working with the coach is so powerful that it overshadows what the individual may learn in any other setting. Research has shown that people do more or less what is expected of them.

Summary

- A skill is a physical and emotional process having a positive outcome.
- Coaches have a role to play in helping the individual to identify the physical process; to understand the emotion barriers; and to combine physical enhancement with emotional building so that a positive outcome can be achieved.
- We all have innate abilities. Through coaching people become aware of the skills they can acquire through practice, until the new skill becomes equally innate.
- Reaching plateaux of performance and having setbacks is normal.
- Both coach and the person being coached need to be wary of the danger and opportunity zone. Dependent upon their knowledge and acceptance of a reduction of performance while new skills are being learnt, the person being coached can either return to old levels of performance, or reach potential higher levels of achievement.
- Learning from mistakes is a poor substitute for good coaching.
- There is a time to 'tell'—the trick is knowing when it is appropriate. There are some things which act as rules—sometimes there is only one to way to do something. It would be inappropriate to allow someone to come to harm, physically or emotionally, just to prove a point.
- Individuals being coached have a personal responsibility to improve their own performance.
- Coaches can be directive and cajole people into repeating their performance until they get it right. It depends on how it is done.
- A manager's and a coach's expectations of an individual can have a dramatic effect on the outcome, for better and for worse. Negative expectations bring about negative results. Positive expectations bring about positive results.
- We have a tendency to treat differently those performing at lower levels than others, and in such a way as to accelerate the negative effects of the self-fulfilling prophesy.

Recommended reading

Bass, B.M. (1981) *Leadership and Performance Beyond Expectations*. Free Press.
Brown, R. (1988) *Group Processes*. Blackwell.
Festinger, Leon (1957) *A Theory of Cognitive Dissonance*. Stanford University Press.
Janis, I.L. (1971) 'Groupthink', *Psychology Today*, November.
Livingston, J.S. (1969) 'Pygmallion in management', *Harvard Business Review*. July/August.

Morgan, Clifford T. (1961) *Introduction to Psychology*. McGraw-Hill, 2nd edn.

Racham, N. and Morgan, T. (1977) *Behaviour Analysis in Training*. McGraw-Hill.

Single, J.L. (1980) 'Productivity and the self-fulfilling prophecy', *Management World*. November.

Stewart, V. and Stewart, A. (1981) *Business Applications of Repertory Grid*. McGraw-Hill.

5 The major problems in adopting a coaching programme and how to overcome them

This chapter examines the main reasons that managers either believe or perceive to be the obstacles in the way of operating a coaching philosophy and suggests discussion points aimed to overcome them. It ends with an examination of the problems all of us face in accepting change.

Obstacles to adoption of a coaching philosophy

If you were to ask your managers what they would see to be the main difficulties they would face in introducing a coaching philosophy, the list would probably look like this:

1 They do not believe it is their responsibility to coach staff.
2 They perceive that they do not have the time to coach their staff.
3 They are no good at coaching their staff.
4 Managers are unaware of the benefits of coaching.
5 Managers are not rewarded for coaching activity.
6 In order to become a coach, managers have to change their style of leadership.
7 They believe they are doing it already.

Each item needs to be dealt with separately, and I would suggest the following discussion points.

It is not the manager's job

There is nothing new in the suggestion from me that unless you have support for the coaching ethos from the top, then the chances are that it will not work. Not being new, however, does not make it any the less relevant. Almost all company initiatives fail because senior managers say one thing and do another. If they happen to say and do the same things then so much the better. So if included in the company's objectives is a policy of adopting coaching as a principal management activity, then *all* managers will have to adopt the principles.

Ask your senior managers:

If you told your staff that due to financial pressures, the company could no longer afford to run the staff canteen, and then got external caterers in to provide for the managers, what would the effect be on staff performance?

If we implement a coaching philosophy, whereby managers coach their immediate subordinates, but the managers themselves were not coached by you, how committed would those managers be to the coaching philosophy?

When it comes to the first-line managers themselves, we have already looked at what they believe the traditional role of a manager is, and the list included such activities as:

- Planning
- Delegating
- Motivating
- Decision making
- Leading

To reinforce the point already made about how many of these tasks could be replaced by either computers or an administrator, in the same way that we broke down the subordinate job into segments, the process could be used here to describe in specific terms the managerial function. For example, in the area of planning, you could get the managers to discuss what is involved in planning. The items produced could be:

- Preparing budgets
- Analysing manpower requirements
- Forecasting sales
- Time management
- Preparing reports

While all laudable functions, they are hardly the stuff of operational managers. Propose the following questions:

What would be the effect on team performance if you were ill for two months? If you left the company, and were not replaced, what effect would it have on the company's performance?

The last question for most managers is extremely unpalatable and yet they know full well what the answer is.

Your purpose should be to assist managers in understanding that their primary function is in interactive interventions with their staff that bring about changes and improvement in performance. Many managers are concerned that in becoming coaches they have to be trainers. To do this they have to know the job inside out. A lot of managers move from a particular job to eventually manage others in the same job, and can over a period of time lose touch with the practicality of that occupation, other than an historical appreciation of it. Some managers may not have done the job themselves. Whatever the situation, managers do not have to do the job to coach others in it, and that is a major learning point for them. In the case study material in Chapter 8, you will see examples of coaching sessions, where it is plainly evident that the manager is a catalyst, not a demonstrator. In this early selling period of the coaching ethos you should arrange for the demonstration of a skill, by someone unskilled in the actual job, very much along the lines shown in the case studies in Chapter 8, and I have included a particular one that could be shown—

using snooker to experience coaching. Your problem will be solved when your first group of managers become devotees to coaching. There are no greater disciples than converts.

As part of this continuing discussion, ask:

What is it that you could do as a manager, that would make it very difficult to replace you?

In the main, the *only* reason for a first-line manager has to be that he or she actively contributes towards an increased performance of the individual.

There is not enough time to coach

Coaching does not have to be a full day with an individual. It can last five minutes. It can last a full week. The determinant of time spent on the process is a matter of negotiation between coach and the person being coached. Managers are great complainers that there is a lack of time available to do all of the things they are supposed to do, but in that, they are no different from anyone else.

One of your initial jobs with the senior management group is to define how much time managers should be spending in coaching activities. My advice is that it should represent 60 per cent of their available time. With the senior management group, work out what are the things that line managers get involved in which stop them spending at least 60 per cent of their time in coaching activities, and stop them.

Some research shows that many top managers actually spend their time in far less structured activities than previously assumed. It has been said that senior executives spend most of their time in short exchanges with all levels of staff, making themselves available for others to bounce ideas off, and to ask others questions about their activities. This questioning is not done in a threatening manner, but more in a style which shows interest. Yet in most time management training sessions it is normal to teach managers that other people are time wasters and that you should create barriers and systems stopping them getting to you. That is why those people slavishly adhering to these systems eventually become totally divorced from reality and effectiveness.

With all managers, especially first-line managers themselves, it is highly likely, just as it is with the rest of the population, that what one person sees as a lot of available time, another feels is not time enough. It is a fact of life that some people achieve twice as much in half the time. A simple exercise to display how perception of time differs between people is to ask managers to stand up, put their hands behind their backs, not look at any watch or clock, and to sit down again when they believe one minute of time has elapsed. Having carried out this session hundreds of times I can guarantee that the first person will most likely sit down after about 35 seconds, and the last person will sit down after about 90 seconds. Over the period of 24 hours that could be an astonishing difference in the perception of the same available time. It is not the time available that makes the difference, it is what different people do with that time.

Ask your managers:

If you were in the middle of a major project, and you were told by your boss that you now had only half as much time left to finish the project as was originally agreed, and that finishing it well would dictate your promotional prospects, would you finish the project?

Even though it is a pressure question, that most would feel aggrieved to comply with, in reality, most would finish the project within the new time-scale. Work, it is said, expands to fill the time set aside to accomplish it.

Time is a commodity that all managers have equal quantities of, but obviously how managers use that time dictates how effective or successful they are. It depends on how your organization measures success.

Some companies have spent a considerable amount of money introducing time management systems, sending managers on courses to learn how to use their time more effectively. In some cases the seniority of the manager determines the quality of the time management system distributed on these courses. Top managers get kid leather systems, middle managers get plain leather systems, and the rest get plastic-backed systems—it certainly does a lot for staff–manager relationships and I have yet to see any that works.

One of the best books on time management I have read is Alan Lakien's *How to Get Control of Your Time and Your Life*. It is full of common sense things to do. I especially like the comments about organizing paperwork into 'A's, 'B's and 'C's. He advocates throwing 'C's in the waste bin, saying that if it is important it will come around again. I have never looked back, and my waste bin floweth over.

It does not matter what you do on time management training, you can either prove that there is plenty of time to coach, or the manager will prove that there is not. It has nothing to do with time, it has to do with desire. Those people that want to, will. As we have already discussed, everyone has a totally different perception of time, and no amount of time management training, and time management systems will change that. I recall one particular manager I worked with once who was paranoid about time management. He had been on one of the courses I mentioned and had the executive version—a kid leather diary. It was always full. Every second of his work life was accounted for, and it was probably the same at home. When I tried to see him one day—I only needed a minute—his secretary stopped me:

Have you an appointment?

It's all right I just need to see him for a minute. Is he in?

He can't see you without an appointment. He's tied up now for three days. You could see him on Thursday.

I left it. It wasn't important enough to me to make an appointment. The same man used to write memos to me. If he stood on his chair and peered over the screens in the office he could see me. Time eventually caught up with him and he was replaced for being totally ineffective. He was very adept at managing time, but at the end of the day he was still useless.

You cannot teach people how to manage time, you might only be able to make them aware about how much time they waste. Unless, however, they have clear goals and the commitment to take the first step towards achieving them. I recommend that you spend more time on goal setting than on time management.

Set a task, that each manager has to give a two minute presentation on setting goals, and how to achieve them. The learning points that will emerge will become self-evident. People know what they have to do, they simply never get around to it. One humorous way of tackling this is, before you begin the session, cut out a number of circles with the word 'tuit' written in the centre of each. At the end hand them out saying:

I notice that many of you have goals which you say have not been achieved because you have not got around to it. Here is a round 'tuit' for each of you, so now what's stopping you?

Managers rarely have the level of skill needed to coach

I propose that managers do have the necessary level of skill, but it is likely to be well hidden. So to unearth it requires time, perseverance and practice. Nothing can substitute for practice, and as practice will take time, you have to have full senior management support of the continuance of coaching as a company process. Whether cosmetic or not, you should publish a five-year coaching plan, with a proviso that each year it will be updated. Managers and staff need to feel that coaching is not just another nine-day wonder, and sight of a five-year plan should give them some confidence in the fact that coaching is here to stay. Publishing a five-year plan also flushes out your senior managers' commitment, as alongside the plan will be the allocation of resources.

Coaching in one sense is merely the skill of questioning, and it is therefore reasonable to assume that even the worst of managers can be trained to ask questions. The real level of skill arrives when the manager knows what the right question is to ask, at the right time, and can cope with the answer. I recall learning to speak French at school, where I became very proficient at saying the right things, and at asking questions in French; the problem was, when I used it in France, people answered back. The questions I understood, the answers I received remain to this day a mystery. As with all other skills training, you have to get your managers to use a prescriptive form of questions, such as those in the next chapter, until they have a good set of their own which also work.

The resistance can be substantial, but you will have to stick to your guns. In your early discussions with senior managers, you need to explain that the process of coaching skill acquisition will require constant practice, that it will be resisted, but that it is also the only way to achieve eventual successful use of the technique.

For example, people are not allowed to drive the car any way they want when they are learning. The instructor has a pre-set method of learning which everyone has to follow. Later, when people have learnt to drive, they improve, or in some cases deteriorate! Some go on to be champion drivers, others simply use the skill to travel, but many of the basics will remain. The same processes are in play when learning coaching skills, it is just that people appear to find the analogy difficult to understand. Skills in which we use our verbal dexterity are similar to the skills in which we use our physical dexterity. For most, however, the link between practice and skill improvement is easier to understand when applied to an athletic skill, than when applied to verbal skills. They are, nevertheless, the same.

Most managers initially make bad coaches because they are too used to being managers. Your job is to sell them the personal benefit of being a coach.

It is also usual for people to feel as though they are being cloned if you prescribe the actual words to use, as in the POWER model. I find this excuse to learning something new extremely tiresome. It appears to me sometimes that some people believe they invented the language and invented the way to respond to it. We are conditioned to respond. A good way to demonstrate this is to ask people to get a blank sheet of paper and give them the following set of instructions:

I will call out a series of statements asking you to write something down. You must write down what immediately comes into your mind, and do it very quickly, as I will be moving on at considerable speed. For example if I say to you 'A type of cloth' you may write down 'cotton' or 'tea' or 'wool', etc.

Once they understand what you want them to do call out the following:

1 A colour
2 A flower
3 A piece of furniture
4 A number between one and four
5 The name of an animal in the zoo
6 A tree in the wood
7 A vegetable

I have done this simple test a number of times, and the chances are extremely high, that most people will pick the answers to be:

1 Red
2 Rose
3 Chair
4 Three
5 Lion
6 Oak
7 Carrot

Why? Because most of these objects are pictures that we learnt at school and they come out when triggered. While not scientific, in general terms, behaviour of this sort is predictive. In the same way that asking the questions in the POWER model will in most cases produce a predictive response—self-awareness, personal responsibility and commitment to an agreed action plan.

If I could show you how to predict the outcome of a conversation by learning a series of questions, you would be interested in looking at that wouldn't you? My prediction is that most of you will have said yes.

Managers are unaware of the personal benefits of coaching

I propose that it is highly likely that many managers do not like managing people. They like the *idea* of managing people, they like the title 'manager', they like the status of management, but they do not like the daily grind of managing people. Listen to any group of managers relaxing, and I promise that you will not hear anyone who says:

It's great to be a manager.

Most will complain about the staff, complain about the boss, and complain about the lack of time, money and people.

Managing people badly is a stressful experience, and most managers manage people badly. How do I know? Ask most employees. Ask your managers how they are managed, and what makes them think they are any different?

Being a coach releases managers from the daily grind of managing people. They are still accountable, but it is a far less pressurized environment in which to work. As already explained, getting people to accept personal responsibility for their own performance is a very cathartic process for a manager. Most managers are brought up to believe that they are personally responsible for the failure of their staff. While coaching does not absolve managers of their own responsibilities and overall accountability for the performance of their staff, responsibility is placed both where it belongs and where it is most effective—with the individual employee. Unless each member of staff accepts personal responsibility it is impossible to achieve high performance levels. One of the common factors in those performing at a high level of skill is the fact that they accept personal responsibility for their performance levels.

Also, managers have a habit of wanting to be sold the benefit for *them*, whereas a way to approach it may be to have them decide what are the benefits for the individual. The person being coached may feel:

- more involved in the process.
- released from a controlling mechanism and therefore enjoy the work better.
- committed to goals.
- a greater sense of achievement because his or her manager came up with the answer to performance problems.
- the desire to seek help more often from his or her manager.

Therefore, if these and other benefits materialize, what effect will they have on the employee's performance, and correspondingly what benefits will the manager derive?

Managers are not rewarded for coaching activity

Managers tend to be rewarded, either for maintaining procedures or for bottom line results. I am not against bottom line results, but the focus of the bottom line will have a tendency to polarize performance between success and failure. In most work teams the 80/20 principle rules: 80 per cent of successful performance comes from 20 per cent of the workforce. Even though most people, therefore, fail to deliver what companies may determine to be a successful performance, managers always point to the successful 20 per cent as being role models for those not performing. Companies need to appreciate that most of those 20 per cent are successful in spite of management. They are the ones who will tend to succeed no matter what the environment.

In this simple approach to work, of believing that the 80 per cent under-performing simply have to be like the 20 per cent performing, managers and the companies they work for fail to appreciate the significant contribution that is most likely made by the 80 per cent and how under-utilized they are. That performance can be radically enhanced through the coaching processes I have outlined so far, but only if managers are encouraged, and rewarded in carrying them out.

Having said that, you should be wary of focusing merely on activity. A focus simply on activity will produce activity. Classically, sales managers have a firm belief that the more people you see, the more successful you will be. This is usually reinforced by the fact that successful salespeople generally see more people than unsuccessful salespeople. What sales managers fail to grasp, is that it does not take a genius to work out that you have to see people to sell. Even those performing at the bottom of the team can work that out for themselves. That does not stop managers setting activity targets for their salespeople. The salesperson quickly learns how to play the activity game, sees lots of people, and stands still in performance terms. Activity is not enough: it is the kind of activity that is important.

You yourself will most likely have examples of people at work who look busy but achieve very little. They walk around with files, have mounds of paperwork on their desks, constantly look under pressure, but when it comes to answering the question:

What do they actually do?

the response can often be:

I haven't a clue.

Most managers are task orientated, and yet coaching relies heavily on being process orientated. Only by focusing on the elements of the process, will it be possible to improve performance, step by step.

Let us look at the example I covered during the whole–part–whole sequence, in which we identified an element of successful performance as being the use of sales aids, and the component parts of that element were as follows:

- Having a presenter.
- The presenter is clean.

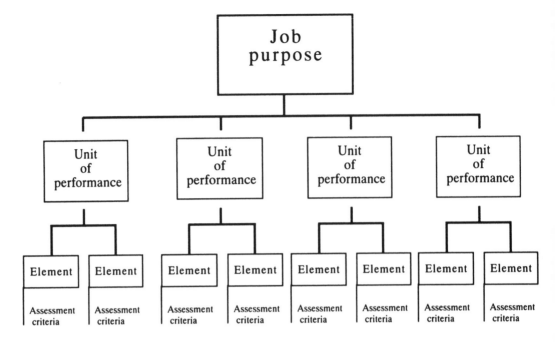

Figure 5.1 *Competency-based approach to identifying job performance factors*

- The sales aids are uncluttered.
- The sales aid is used interactively.
- The sales aid is not given to the customer, but shown and explained.

If your managers adopt the competency-based approach to identifying job performance factors, it is possible to develop a list of items that can be used as a method for managers to focus on specific items that contribute to the whole performance.

The competency-based approach to identifying performance factors is a methodology whereby the job is broken down into major units, the elements that make up those units, the performance factors that subsequently contribute to the performance of those elements, and a list of criteria which managers can assess in the field (Figure 5.1).

If we take the example of using sales aids, the unit could be described as follows:

1 *Major unit* Using sales aids.
2 *Elements* The elements that make up the major unit of job performance could be:
  (a) Prepare sales aids which are relevant to the presentation.
  (b) Describe product features with the use of sales aids which are easily understood by the customer.
  (c) Keep sales aids in a condition which enhances presentation.
  (d) Use the sales aid in an interactive process which involves the customer.

3 *Performance standards* From these elements it is then possible to draw up a range of performance standards:

Sales aids comply with company standards and procedures; they are jargon free; they are clean and tidy and kept available to use when appropriate; they are in the form of pre-printed format or computer images; the client is encouraged to discuss the benefits of the products being shown.

4 *Assessment criteria* Lastly, it is possible to determine a range of assessment criteria which the manager can focus on in the field:
   (a) The salesperson prepared a range of sales aids to be used in a presentation.
   (b) The sales aids used were of a high standard and kept available for use when needed.
   (c) The salesperson explained the product to the customer and used language which avoided jargon. Checked that the customer understood.

This is obviously only an example of the sort of process that you could adopt with your own products and services and with your own managers. The point is, that by identifying the specific standards of performance that you expect of managers, you may be able to reward the behaviour, if observed, which leads to employee success.

The manager has to change management style to that of a coach

The most difficult thing you can ask anyone to do, it seems, is to change. Managers, more than any other group of workers, resist change. In this scenario, asking them to give up their normal management style to encompass true coaching and empowering their staff will require patience and perseverance.

A good place to start is to explain to managers how normal it is to resist change. Also, by sharing with them the process of change which I will now describe, it will help their self-awareness. If you know what is happening to you, it becomes easier to cope.

The process of change is viewed in five stages. When faced with forced change, each of us tends to go through all five stages, and in many ways, we have to. Missing out a stage can leave issues unresolved, and it is noticeable that those who either say that experiencing each stage is unnecesssary or that a particular stage is irrelevant, often end up back in the process of change, not accepting the inevitable. I also believe that in most cases the process is sequential—you have to move from one to another in a logical, and as it turns out, emotional succession. This does not mean, however, that once dealt with a stage has been completed. People often return to a previous stage, until eventually it has been resolved.

The five stages of forced change are:

1 Denial
2 Anger
3 Bargaining
4 Depression
5 Acceptance

It would probably be easier to understand the stages of change by relating a classic example of a situation which happened to me a couple of years ago when I was working in the insurance division of a large financial institution. The building my department was in was to be renovated, and some 600 people in total had to be relocated to other offices, five miles away, for a period of at least six months.

Although faced with immediate change, and not being too keen about the prospect and the disruption, the actual move was quickly resolved for most staff. It is possible to go through all the phases of change very quickly:

I can't believe they want us to move out [denial]. It's a disgrace. How am I supposed to work under these conditions [anger]? What about if we left it until I finish this project [bargaining]? It's no good, the project will suffer, it's a disaster [depression]. OK, I can't do anything about it, let's get on with it [acceptance].

When we got to our new premises, however, the five stages of change took considerably longer to be resolved. The first thing that happened to me was that I was separated from my colleagues, and put into an area in another part of the building with other managers, in what was euphemistically called a 'pig-pen'—a small area with a desk, a chair, a cupboard and three screens. It was possible, though quite athletic, to touch all the boundaries without moving.

1 *Denial*

I can't believe this. This has to be a mistake.

I telephoned the person responsible for allocating space.

John, I've got a problem here, I've been put in an area where I shouldn't be.

I explained the situation. It was right. This was where I had to be. I sat down.

No this can't be right.

I telephoned someone else. It was right.

No, this can't be right, it doesn't make sense.

Much of the first day was spent checking it out.

2 *Anger* Day two.

I'm not having this.

I went to the area where my staff were. For the rest of the day they ran for cover as I stomped around.

This is ridiculous. I can't work in these conditions. Who do they think they are? This place is a mess. Get it cleaned up. How much space have you got? You don't need all this space. Where am I going to put my books? What have you done about fixing the computer line up?

The point about anger is that while releasing frustration in some way, it is a fruitless activity with only negative consequences. For a short while it made me feel better, but it hardly enhanced staff relations.

3 *Bargaining* The next day I walked around the building, and on the next floor up found an empty office, and another next to it with stationery in it.

John, there's an empty office on the next floor up, can I have that? Oh I see. Well the one next door only has stationery in it. If I got it moved, could I use that as an office?

I was told that it would be needed in two months by another department.

Well, that's OK, I'll move again later.

The idea wasn't well received. I approached my manager.

Peter I need your help.

It didn't work. I went back to my secretary.

Mary, what about if we moved you and Julie into that space, and I moved into this one? Alan, if you got rid of that equipment, and turned your desk around we could have a bit of space here. You know, this office for three of you is full of cupboards. If we put them into storage, I could have this office.

Nothing worked.

This is just stupid [back to anger]. There must have been a mistake [denial].

It turns out there was. I was missed off the original plans—my fault.

I don't believe it [denial]. Well somebody better get their finger out [anger]. As I was missed off the original plans, and wasn't supposed to be here anyway, obviously I need to be where I was supposed to be [bargaining].

Nothing worked.

4 *Depression* Day four arrived. I sat in the space. All around me was noise. I was surrounded by about 1000 people.

I can't work here. This is awful. This is impossible. It's dreadful. My work will suffer. The project might as well be binned. Why me?

Mary came in to see me.

Look at this place—it's a mad house [anger]. I can't believe this is happening [denial and depression]. What about if we moved the desk the other way around [bargaining]?

It was moved. It was not any better.

It's worse [depression]. I want to know who missed me off the plans [anger].

It was my boss.

I knew it. It's outrageous [anger]. But nobody's going to change their mind—it's hopeless [depression].

5 *Acceptance* Day five.

This is pointless. I can't do anything about it. It's a case of like it or lump it, but I've got a job to do.

I worked late for a month making up the wasted time. Finished the project to schedule. When we moved back to the original building six months later, my office had disappeared—

I don't believe it!

Developing management awareness of the process

Before sharing the full model with managers, ask them the last time they experienced a state of denial or disbelief; then separately anger; then bargaining, depression, and acceptance. By building up the discussion, and by asking the question 'What happened next?' your managers will themselves bring up the five stages of change.

If you know the stages, it becomes easier to handle the process. The sooner each of us gets to acceptance the better. That does not mean, however, that for most of us just accepting the situation works. Most of us have to go through the process. Realizing what the process is, however, helps us and also helps us to recognize what is happening to others.

They say they do it already

A common situation, with which I have been confronted, is that managers say that they already adopt a coaching style. In fact one of the most difficult cases with which I dealt was a manager who steadfastly refused training as a coach, saying that he completely understood the coaching philosophy. In reality he was probably the worst coach I have seen, and yet by not taking part in any of the self-awareness training inherent in developing managers as coaches, he was oblivious to his lack of technique. The only saving grace for me was that his team consistently under-performed. As we have already discussed, many managers have a far higher self-perception of their ability than is actually the case. So how do you cope, and what can you do about it? The fact is that no manager will change unless he or she wants to. Even those that are performing badly will tend to blame the staff rather than themselves, and those that accept that the fault lies with themselves sometimes find it impossible to change. All I can say is that you simply cannot win everybody over and along the way there will be some casualties. With the dialogue you have hopefully built up with the senior management team, you might be able to identify the problem, but then many senior managers are also loath to censure or to change first-line managers. Their view could be that once the rot sets in and managers are forced to change or are disciplined, where could it end?

The only way to convince the Doubting Thomases is to have disciples. You must concentrate on a few managers who embrace your views and work with them to improve the performance of their teams.

Summary

- Managers can resist the coaching ethos because they perceive that it is not their responsibility, they do not have enough time, they lack the skills, they are not rewarded for coaching activity, they are unaware of the benefits of coaching, they would have to change their style of leadership, and many believe they are doing it already.
- To overcome these points you need to elicit total senior management

support for coaching; have the coaching philosophy included in long-term training plans and objectives; ensure that managers are rewarded for processes as well as end product; focus on the benefits for individuals being coached, not coaches; and understand that time is not the issue but desire.

- One of the biggest obstacles is the resistance to change of any kind. One way to alleviate this is to make people aware of the five stages of forced change: denial, anger, bargaining, depression, and acceptance. Help managers cope with this predictable reaction to change.
- A major way of convincing managers of the benefits of coaching is to work hard in gaining a disciple among the management group.

Recommended reading

Fletcher, Shirley (1991) *NVQs: Standards and Competence*. Kogan Page, London.

Godefroy, Christian H. and Clark, John (1989) *The Complete Time Management System*. Judy Piatkus, London.

Lakien, Alan (1984) *How to Get Control of Your Time and Your Life*. Gower, Aldershot.

Parkinson, C. Northcote (1957) *Parkinson's Law*. John Murray, London.

6 Power coaching

This chapter proposes an easy to remember model which trainers and managers can use during coaching sessions to keep on track—'POWER'. The model is expanded to include specific questions which coaches can ask and which will release solutions to performance problems from those being coached.

A model— POWER coaching

The dictionary describes power as the ability to do or to act. It characterizes energy and vigour and something which has an active property. We talk about people who have power, either as a result of being given it due to a position of authority, or of taking it. It has become synonymous with force, rather than with strength, although in many ways, the power that is normally exerted over us by others, could involve an implied threat of strength being used.

I use the word power in a positive sense. I see power as being the life-force which exists in most people, and something which can be translated into constructive endeavour. I see coaching as returning power to individuals. The problem is that we enter the world as powerless, and while the possibilities open to us are endless, the realization of those opportunities relies heavily on our being given power by others in order to act. In the processes of growing, of learning, and of being cared for, ruled, controlled or directed, that return or empowerment of our personal power can sometimes fail to emerge. The more civilized the society, the greater the number of rules. We began with Ten Commandments. It is said that we now have 35 million laws. It is small wonder that people have lost the ability to think for themselves, and more importantly act for themselves. I tend to agree with Samuel Smiles, who in 1859 said:

Whatever is done *for* men or classes, to a certain extent takes away the stimulus and necessity for doing for themselves; and where men are subjected to over-guidance and over-government, the inevitable tendency is to render them comparatively helpless.

As part of your coaching programme for managers I recommend that each be given Smiles's book *Self Help* as standard reading.

Some people may feel uncomfortable with the use of the word 'power'. Certainly it can have sinister connotations. Power in the wrong hands can be dangerous, both mentally and physically. Coaches can and often do become a powerful focus for the people they are coaching. They can in some cases appear very charismatic, and as such can exude omnipotent influence. Like patients with their doctors, people being coached can often become infatuated with the coach who releases them. It is something to be wary about and is discussed in greater depth in Chapter 8. For now, let it be said, that using power coaching techniques can be, and has been seen to be, of enormous benefit to both coaches and the people they are coaching. The end result of successful power coaching is to reach fulfilment—completing the POWER acronym to POWERFUL.

Transferring theory to practice

I have found that one of the contributory reasons why managers at times appear unable to transfer theory into practice is the lack of workable tools to use in the field. What seems like a good idea on a training course dissipates with the reality of employing the theory face to face with staff. Recently, when I was training a group of senior managers in a large life assurance company, the managing director summed up the feelings of her colleagues by saying:

This is the first process of developing and empowering people that not only makes sense but also contains a practical model which gives me the confidence to use it.

All managers want is something which they can quickly learn, which is easy to use, and which works. POWER coaching achieves all of this. As I have said, the purpose of coaching is to release talent by the intervention of the coach. The process used is one of structured questioning. The model has a structure to it, and, while I am against slavish adherence to any managerial tool, sticking to the POWER structure whenever possible does give the coaching session, whatever the time period, a direction with a clearly defined beginning, middle and end. I have found that many conversations, training sessions and discussions between managers and employees often end up in limbo, not because the desire to help is missing, but because there rarely appears to be a structure. My feedback from using POWER is that it helps managers as much as it helps employees.

POWER stands for *Purpose, Objectives, What is happening now?, Empowering,* and *Review*. Using this as a framework, coaching becomes a series of structured questions which initially are prescriptive, in the sense that they should be asked in sequential order. However, it will become evident in the later stages of the model that both coach and trainee may need to return to the earlier elements of the model to seek clarification, especially of the goal. The model is simple to remember, and with practice can be delivered in an easy conversational style. That ease belies the powerful nature of its potential impact. I have reproduced the model at the end of this chapter so that you can copy it for managers and yourself to use in the field, until such time as you can remember the main questions to use.

Purpose

The first part of the model is concerned with defining the *purpose* of the coaching session. That is to say, what is it possible to achieve within the time available? It would be usual for most people to go straight into defining objectives, and from my experience, it is the lack of clarification of the purpose and parameters of the coaching sessions that causes many people to stumble at the first hurdle. Having an unclear purpose for the coaching session even before defining goals, is like flying off into the fog and then later deciding on a destination. In any case, the process of questioning the purpose of the session in itself prepares people psychologically to take part in what is to come.

Both parties need to agree at the outset what they are trying to achieve, not in terms of goals, or end results, but within the parameters of the coaching session. In this way, both the person being coached and the coach have a purpose, but the purpose of the former must take precedence. The individual, therefore, has ownership of the overall purpose. A component of agreeing the parameters of the session is also to concede the possible limitations of the event. Only so much can be achieved in any one session. Both parties need time to consolidate any learning or performance improvement accomplished. The person being coached has to practise the new skill or improvement, and the coach has to observe the progress being made. That is not to say that coaching sessions are short. Nor are they long. The purpose has to be agreed at the beginning. That purpose, however, should not be too ambitious. It takes time for new learning to be embedded, and it is all too common to attempt to push ahead too quickly because things are going well, only for the improvement to fade away within hours of the event. Tackling too much too soon should be avoided.

As in counselling, it is important to demarcate who has responsibility for what. Individuals need to understand the limitations of the session, both in terms of available time, and of the potential goals to be tackled.

Questions to ask   • *How much time have we got?* The response to this question should be followed by the coach establishing what is feasible within the time-scale. For example,

> COACH   Obviously 30 minutes will only allow us to get a feel of what we are trying to help you achieve, and it is highly likely that we may have to schedule a further time slot soon to take this initial discussion a stage further. Are you comfortable with that?

If it is a later coaching session, where some work has already been achieved, then both coach and individual will have become used to establishing the parameters relating to time. Be careful that through familiarity with any or all parts of the process that you are not tempted to skip parts of it assuming that the individual knows the rules of the game. It is always dangerous to assume and the fundamental precept is that ideally each part of the process should be adhered to on each occasion. Use the term 'we' whenever possible. Much of the coaching session is a shared responsibility.

The only time when 'we' is inappropriate is at the point where the person being coached has to do something. 'Doing' is that person's responsibility. Later in the model, when action is being sought, it would be inappropriate for the coach to say:

What are we going to do now?

At that stage, once action had been agreed it would be a case of:

What are you going to do now?

- *What is the purpose of this session for you?* The person being coached must articulate the purpose of the session. It is not for the coach to decide the purpose, even if the coach believes that the purpose of the session might more usefully be something else.

  That said, if the individual being coached comes up with a purpose which the coach does not feel would add value to performance, the validity of the individual choice can be questioned. For example,

  COACH How will this add value to your overall performance?

  Having received a reply to this, however, the coach should then back off. By pushing further, the coach may intimidate the individual into saying exactly what the coach wants to hear. Coaching technique in the wrong hands can be manipulative. Manipulation merely results in the coach's aims and objectives being realized, and while the people being coached may enjoy short-term benefit, it is rarely sustainable. Classically, the charismatic trainer will elicit commitment during a training event, which eventually is weakened by the passage of time.

- *What are you looking for from me?* The coach needs to establish from the person being coached what he or she believes the relationship is to be. We have already said that the relationship is different from that of client and counsellor. At some stage the coach may direct, and not necessarily with kid gloves. Coaches have objectives to achieve too.

  If what is expected from the coach is thought to be unreasonable, for example within the time-scale, then the coach is entitled to say so. All matters of a performance issue come from the trainee. The coach may very well be a major influence, but performance comes from within. The coach may motivate, but the trainee may remain unmotivated. Some coaches have unrealistically high expectations of their powers of persuasion.

These early sessions, whether they are the beginning of a coaching programme or represent an element in the middle or end, are central to the success of coaching. Get this wrong, and it will all go wrong. More time should be spent defining the relationship and establishing goals, than probably in coaching itself.

Objectives and options Purists may argue that there is a difference between objectives and goals. The point could be debatable, but is not for debate here. Most people at the receiving end cannot tell the difference, and coaching is about acknowledging the existence of the recipient, not the giver. I therefore use the term 'objectives' equally to mean 'goals', simply because most people understand them to be so.

An inability to clarify objectives is like having an open lifetime journey ticket, and leaving the destination up to the driver, while you, the passenger, sit passively in the back seat. People spend considerably more time planning their holidays than they spend planning their lives. Defining objectives, whether of the complete coaching programme, or of deciding the objective of all of the work, and of long-term goals, is of equal importance. Each leads to the next, and is reliant upon getting the first step right. Getting off on the wrong foot can have disastrous results. Some would say that Colin Jackson lost his chance of the gold medal in the Barcelona Olympics of 1992, not because he could not hurdle, but because his focus was purely on the end purpose. He was desperate to win the gold medal. All he could think about was crossing the tape and winning. It could be argued that he focused too far ahead. When Linford Christie was asked after his gold winning 100 m run what he had been thinking about seconds before the race, he replied— 'Getting up'. Sally Gunnell, another gold medal winner in a comparable race to Jackson, said she focused on the steps in between each hurdle. As she sensed a problem, she changed leg, something she had practised for three years, and in so doing kept her race winning momentum going. Jackson's immediate goal, it can be assumed, was to win, when a more worthwhile immediate goal might have been to get up, then to run an exact number of steps, and to clear each hurdle. As it was, he began hitting hurdles almost immediately. Winning was so obvious an end goal, that once having decided it, it then becomes obsolete apart from regularly updating.

At work, some people concentrate too much on the end result, or are obsessed so much with 'what-ifs' that they fail to start off right, and subsequently fail to complete a task effectively. All sorts of jobs suffer from the 'running before walking' syndrome, and it is all part of the 'I want it, and I want it now' culture. The coach's role is not to slow down progress but to ensure that progress is maintained towards an end goal. If anything, the coach's eye is on the end goal all of the time. That is the coach's job; it is not the performer's. This becomes the relationship between the performer and the coach. The coach holds the end goal on behalf of the performer. However, it still belongs to the performer. It is like depositing a goal into a performance bank, where the coach is the cashier. Every now and then the coach lets the performer know how much interest has accrued, and how far it is to the end goal. The performer may at any time change the end goal, that is not the coach's choice. The coach merely keeps the performer on track and informed. In the working environment, therefore, the relationship is the same. People, with the help of the coach, decide what it is they want to do, and how they intend to achieve it, in steps from the immediate to the long term.

Defining the immediate objective before beginning is vital. Most people have some idea what the long-term, or even medium-term goal is. Where they have problems is with the immediate goal. Sometimes, standing too close to the goal is taken so much for granted that it tends to be overlooked. It is so close as to be obvious, and therefore we give it our least attention in planning, preparation and visualization. Each journey begins with the first step. That first step leads to another, and eventually the destination. The beauty of taking things one step at a time, however, is that with each success along the journey, the eventual destination also moves, and goals become more and more ambitious. In any event, the journey for many people is just as rewarding as the destination.

The coach's job is to help define the immediate objective and hoped-for outcome of the coaching session, and then to break that down into its component parts. This may take time, and indeed it should if done properly. It should never be taken for granted that the person being coached understands the objective of the session, and the coach must not be intimidated by the exasperation of that person as that immediate objective is sought. The important thing at all times is that the coach and person being coached have to build a trusting relationship which allows each to express himself or herself freely. If an individual has a difficulty in determining the immediate goal the coach should be able to say:

The worst thing here would be for me to suggest a purpose for you. It's a sure fire recipe for you to feel disappointed if you achieve it because it wasn't your purpose, and for me to feel disappointed if you don't. There are no winners unless you determine the purpose.

Questions to ask
- *What are you trying to achieve?* It may take some time to establish the real goal. It could even be that the person being coached has no clear idea of what he or she is trying to achieve. In work environments it can be usual for individuals not to have clear personal goals. The organization may or may not set out its corporate mission; the department may or may not have quality standards, or a shared vision; and the line manager may or may not in a magnetic way influence a picture of future achievement. For the coach, sometimes getting the individual to identify the existence of a personal goal can be a frustrating search.

  As I have already said, we are very used to being told what, when, where and how to do things. Faced with the opportunity to determine our own strategy for life it is hardly surprising that most people do not know where to start, and indeed fail to see why they should.

  A good supplementary question might be:
- *Is this your goal, or someone else's?* It might be argued that someone else's goals, such as the company's or the manager's, is also the subordinate's goal. The goal might be the company target. Unless, however, the employee takes personal ownership of the goal, then coaching will have no effect. If it is the manager's goal, then there will be a need to explore how achieving the manager's goal will help along the journey to the individual's goal. It may be, and probably usually is, of paramount importance that people have the support of their manager. Life is certainly easier when the manager feels in charge. We all of us

learn very quickly how to please figures of authority. What is important is to achieve organizational goals willingly. The practice of resistance becomes so innate, that we also end up resisting our own development sometimes. If you find that the goal is someone else's then you should ask:

- *How can you make it your goal?* It is important that the individual takes personal ownership of any objective. It is pointless continuing the coaching session if the employee persists in saying that he or she has no choice in determining the goal. In some cases the employee may say that his or her goal is to achieve the company target, which is all right, provided that the trainee accepts the fact that there is a choice whether or not to perform. There are obviously consequences in not performing to the company standard, but the choice we all have still remains a personal decision. It is far better for the employee to set a personal objective which is below the target than to accept blindly a given target which he or she personally believes is not achievable. It is worth spending some time reinforcing this point if needed. Certainly, if agreement is not reached about the need for personal acceptance of the objective, long, medium, or short, then you should end the coaching session in order to give both parties the opportunity to rethink the relationship.

Where the employee clearly gives the indication that he or she has not personally accepted the goal, it is permissible for the coach to say:

The lack of acceptance by you of a personal goal, makes it impossible for me to help you reach the performance of which you are capable by coaching. It also throws into doubt your commitment to eventually hitting the company standard. You now have a choice of either coming up with a realistic goal of your own that we can work on, or simply to adopt the normal managerial/subordinate relationship where I tell you what to do, and you either do it or not. Which is it to be?

In some cases, the coach/person being coached relationship can break down, and normal managerial service is resumed. You certainly cannot win them all, and in any event, the whole point about coaching is that individuals have to accept personal responsibility, not just for the achievement of objectives, but also of the coach/person being coached relationship.

We will assume that agreement has been reached, and that we move gracefully on to the next stage.

- *Is this the whole goal, or is it part of something more long term that you want to achieve?* The purpose of this question is to help the individual begin to focus on the first step. All journeys begin with the first step. While that may be, as a colleague of mine said to me recently, a 'BGO' (Blinding Glimpse of the Obvious), sometimes it is easier for people to focus on future distant goals than on the here and now. The here and now implies imminent action. The future requires merely mental commitment. Mental commitment, unless followed up immediately with physical action, will always remain a thought and not a reality.

The coach also needs to know whether the employee has a long-term goal.

Has the employee a purpose? Is this goal merely something to do? Unless he or she defines a purpose the chances of failure are high. More New Year's resolutions are broken than achieved. Not because they aren't good resolutions. Resolutions fail sometimes because the long-term goal has not been established.

People embark upon diets because they want to lose weight. That is a commendable reason. But why? What is the point? Because people do not have a good enough reason, apart from they are fat, or cannot get into last year's clothes, or it is part of a charity slim, most will, if successful, soon put the weight back on. Because they have no long-term goal, of which losing weight is an integral part, most will fail. And by integral I mean that without losing weight the long-term goal will not be achieved. Short- or medium-term achievement can only be embedded if it contributes to a long-term goal.

For example, writing this book was a long-term goal. That meant being published. Before that I had to find a publisher. I had to have a credible product to sell, both in terms of a manuscript and as a writer. One route I could have taken, among a number of options, was to become professionally qualified in the subject I wanted to write about. Those of us not having studied since leaving school would have to set as a first goal a course of study appropriate to our immediate ability, just to get you into the swing of studying again. So you may go back to night classes at a school or college to take an additional GCSE or something similar. Having achieved that, it may then be possible to undertake an undergraduate management diploma at a college, even if entry was only gained through what they call 'age and experience' (my entry route, though whether more through age than experience is debatable). This process of acquiring qualifications, or possibly credibility, could take a long time, but time is not the point. The point is that all goals are made up of a number of other smaller goals. Each is important in achieving the whole.

The thing to recognize is the continuing importance of the next goal, and that there is always something in the distance to go for. In many ways, the long-term goal is meant never to be achieved. People who succeed, do so, not because they achieve their long-term goals, but because they themselves keep moving the goal-post. By that I mean that should the original long-term goal come on to the horizon, and be in sight, then it is fundamental to goal achievement that another long-term goal is established. Whatever it is, being on the journey is important. Arriving at the destination can sometimes be a let-down.

The planting of a number of seeds also safeguards against crop failure. The most bitter people I know are those whose one and only seed did not grow. It did not materialize, and without it came failure, despondency, or embitterment. The journey towards goal achievement calls into a lot of different ports on the way. Life is about experience. We are who we are because of our past, and we will be who we want to be by the actions we employ now and in the future.

Sustainable goal achievement is a result of constantly moving the long-term goal. I have spoken to numerous people who upon achieving their long-term goal have said:

I felt terrific when it was over, and yet it didn't last. Somehow, having got there wasn't as good as the struggle I had getting there.

Some achievers go on and do something else. Super-achievers, while still on the journey to the long-term goal, are planning the next journey.

- *What will you feel like when you achieve your goal?*

- *(Can you see yourself achieving your goal?)* All motivation is internal. It may have external influences but the drive comes from within. Either or both of these questions focus on the internal drive. They also seek to create a picture of achievement. If people can see themselves achieving, then the chances of success are greatly enhanced. Visualization of achievement is a powerful ingredient in all those who achieve success. Visualization is like putting a 35 mm slide of achievement into a projector. When you switch on the light, the image of achievement is thrown up on to the screen and becomes so large that you can almost touch it. The coach should encourage the performer to visualize success and to feel the elation of achievement.

I heard a marvellous story some time ago about President Nixon's visit to China, where he was entertained at a reception given in his honour by a pianist who played Western classical music. The performance was superb. Not till later was it revealed that the pianist had been under house-arrest for five years previously and had been denied access to a piano. The crime, under the Cultural Revolution Laws, was to play Western music in preference to Chinese. During those five years, the pianist, a woman in her middle twenties, had practised daily in her mind. That mental practice kept her as accomplished as anyone physically practising. She was able to play as though she had never stopped practising. I hope the story was true.

- *Is there anything else that you could do?* Is the identified goal really it, or has its identification been more to do with the pressure of the coach? Has the identification of the goal been clearly thought through? Is there something else that should be on the table? It could be that beneath the surface another goal lies hidden—the true goal. It might also be the first step, and may seem so obvious to the individual that it has not yet been properly identified and key tasks set.

The coach should help the person being coached to investigate as many options as the individual can think of. Some of these, while not immediately desirable as an alternative, and even realistic for this moment, may provide choices for much later in the process.

Goal setting is not about identifying the one goal. Putting all your faith and energy into just the one goal can be dangerous. One of the goals has to be the major goal, the one which consumes most of the early efforts of the person being coached, but we all need a fall-back position if something goes wrong. That does not mean that we have a lack of commitment or positive attitude. Positive attitude and commitment, however, are simply not enough. Having encountered difficulty in achieving their only goal I have seen people truly believe that positive mental attitude will make things happen, when anyone with half a brain could see it would not. I have heard people say:

I am totally committed to making this work,

when plainly it would not, no matter what the commitment. I may be totally committed to winning the 100 metres gold medal. I may have a tremendous positive attitude about the reality of my winning it. It may have been my lifetime goal. On the day, what happens if the person next to me runs his lifetime best and beats me? We all have to live with ourselves after the event. Having options, planting seeds, developing new goals, all help. It does not make the commitment any the less. It does not reduce the positiveness of attitude. It is not defeatist. It is coping.

People do, however, have to decide for themselves what the alternatives are. It is common at this juncture for the person being coached to ask the coach what he or she thinks, and perhaps to come up with some alternatives. It is also common for the manager or the trainer to then respond. After all, it is quite flattering to be asked for advice. Most people when asked for advice will give it. There is a danger in responding too early though.

Have you ever given some advice to someone only to have them respond:

Oh I tried that, and it didn't work.

The chances are, that if the individual did not come up with the objective or alternative themselves, the lack of commitment will contribute to failure, thereby reinforcing what a bad idea it was in the first place. Most people fail to reach company targets, not because they are unachievable, but because they have not accepted them. The same is true of options.

The coach can contribute to the generation of options, but only if the ground rules have been set first:

I have got some ideas and some options that you might want to consider, but I stress that they are my ideas. They might not work for you, but if you want to hear them, I can share them with you. The important thing is that I am not recommending any one. The decision as to their acceptability still rests with you.

- *Which course of action do you favour and why?* This is to help the individual decide which is the most favoured course of action. The coach has to be non-judgemental. Whatever the person being coached decides is right, even if it is wrong. By returning to this whole process time and time again, the individual will work out what was right and what was wrong, and what worked and what did not. You may feel that this would take forever, and in the early days it may seem as though it does. However, as with the tortoise and the hare, the best route is not necessarily the fastest.

As with the previous question, the generation of choice is a matter for the individual not the coach. It is also remarkable to observe, no matter how experienced the coach may be in the completion of the task, how different people find different ways of completing the task. Each of them as successful as the other. We all speak differently, although it may be the same language. We all walk differently, even though we all use our legs and feet. We also all see things differently, even though what we see is clearly the same thing. So why cannot we do the job differently? This is the distinction between coaching and training. Training may be prescription in the early stages. The job in its raw form may have to be done in a particular way, and some jobs which involve dangerous processes may always have to be done in the same way. Those sorts of jobs, however, leave no scope for coaching, and in any event performance is measured by a strict compliance to a given set of procedures. The sort of jobs we are looking at should include room for growth, and growth will only be achieved through coaching. Having trained someone to do the basic job to standard, then growth will only be achieved when the individual is released from the shackles of there only being one way to do the job. People must be allowed to express themselves in the work arena in the way in which they feel most comfortable. In the same way that the athlete in the sports arena eventually stands or falls by his or her own performance, so does the performer at work. The athlete will have learnt the basics; been told the rules; have had basic training; but when push comes to shove, in order to express a personal statement beyond that which has been taught, the athlete will need to find his or her own way. The performer at work is the same. The trainer and the manager will help the individual to learn the basics; explain the procedures; and give induction training to do the standard job. To excel at work however, the performer needs to be released to do his or her own thing. We will explore this phenomenon more in 'Empowerment'.

- *When do you want to achieve this goal by?* It is easy enough to talk about having a goal. The true measure of commitment to achieve it is determined by setting a deadline. While the coach may be leading the person being coached to give a commitment, the time is not set by the coach. The coach needs to be able to make an assessment of the potential work involved in helping the individual achieve his or her goal, and to establish whether it is realistic or not. Even so, the answer to realism lies with the individual, and hence the importance of the next question.
- *How realistic is that?* As I said, there is an opportunity for the individual to think again about the realism of committing to a specific time. The coach, from experience, may know how realistic the time-scale is,

but it is not for him or her to comment unless asked. The worst thing a coach can say, and this applies to any stage of the process, is:

Well in my opinion.

These two questions related to time and schedules conclude the goal setting aspect of the model and represent the cornerstone of coaching principles. In my experience, the failure to achieve worthwhile goals has little to do with ability. It has more to do with a lack of vision and planning. The difficulty most of us face is that simply reading the questions to yourself seems not to work. It is their articulation which adds weight and eventually action. As with most goal setting activity, people rarely write their goals down, specify exactly what they mean by them, or set time-scales. We all know the theory. The practice, however, is seldom achieved alone. Herein lies the importance of the coach as a catalyst in the process. The mere fact that an external source asks the questions appears to bring about a positive series of actions.

Having now got into the model, it is worth noting that the elements contained therein, while initially following a predestined course, can and often do retrace steps when one element proves difficult to establish. It would be quite usual for a question such as 'How realistic is that?' to call into doubt the original goal, time-scale, or even relationship of coach and person being coached. Remember too that the coach will have goals. Being a coach is not a vocation, and coaches do not have to sacrifice their own career, aspirations, or even integrity for the greater glory of the person or persons they are coaching. At some stage the coach may decide that the goals, action plans and deadlines are so unrealistic as to warrant a withdrawal. That is not to say that the person being coached may not eventually achieve his or her goal either alone, or with another coach. Also, within work environments, the physical withdrawal of the coach may not be possible or even allowable. But by withdrawal, I use the word in the emotional rather than the physical sense. Remember, earlier in the chapter we discussed how the coach might tackle his or her return to a more traditional managerial role, rather than that of the coach. The decision as to which game is played rests with the person being coached.

What is happening now?

This is a vital part of the process. It could be said that what has gone before is theory. That it is concerned with ideals. 'What is happening now?' is reality. People need to face reality, and in essence that is what true coaching is primarily about. Coaches put people in touch with reality.

Questions to ask:

- *What have you done about it so far?* Has the person being coached really done anything about progressing his or her goal, other than talk about it? I have met numerous people with some fantastic goals. Goals which would, if implemented, set the world alight. Goals which could have changed their lives forever. Goals which never got off the drawing board, because nobody asked the question—'What have you done about it so far?' Merely asking the question can be a spur to action. The problem is, that as individuals, we never ask ourselves this question. That is why the role of the coach is important.

We might talk to ourselves, but if the questions we ask ourselves start becoming tricky, we pretend we did not hear them, or change the question. Even if we ask ourselves:

What have I done about it so far?

we will tend to say:

Actually quite a bit.

Or

Well I haven't had a lot of time.

Or

What was the question?

The coach helps to examine specific actions, not appraising, just asking. The person being coached will know how to judge the response. Faced with someone to ask us the right questions, we do not need judging, we can do that for ourselves. When the trainee says:

I suppose you think . . .

Or

You're probably saying . . .

The coach should reply:

At this stage I have no opinion. What *you* think is more important than my opinion. What do you think?

- *What was the result?* By this stage the person being coached will have opened the floodgates of self-awareness. Talking about our goals, our attempts at starting the journey, and the reality of our experiences is very therapeutic. The focus on reality by the person being coached, merely verbalizing what he or she internally already knows—that the last course of action did not bring the desired results, or that the last course of action failed to deliver all of the results—is enough.

Asking yourself these questions usually pins the blame on someone or something else. Our inner self is very good at coming up with excuses.

I did my best . . . It nearly worked out . . . I didn't get the support . . . The bottom dropped out of the market . . ..

The list can be as long as the time individuals are prepared to talk to themselves. Regardless of the depth of the internal conversation, the fact still remains that it is seldom verbalized. Talking out loud to yourself can land you in serious trouble. Especially if you adopt the full coaching practice, and answer back! We simply do not ask ourselves the right questions. We know what they should be. It just seems that we are unable to vocalize them.

The question facilitates the individual to accept responsibility for the result. There is seldom a need for the coach to say:

And who is responsible for that result?

The danger of doing so is that the individual can then think of someone else who might in his or her opinion actually be responsible for the failure. It is best for the coach to say nothing. A simple shrug will do. The coach needs to be able to display the correct body-language, at the appropriate time. One shrug, a dip of the head, a raising of an eyebrow, and opening of the palms, and a tightening of the lips, will express to the person being coached almost immediately, more than an hour's questioning, what the coach feels.

- *What have been the obstacles?* Examining the obstacles at this stage has two effects. One is that it could save you some considerable time listening to how much other people, events, and the world at large are to blame, and the second is that the person being coached will normally have decided that he or she personally is the biggest obstacle.
- *How did you set about overcoming them?* This reinforces whose responsibility it is to move the process forward. Had the individual taken suitable action before, the session might not be necessary at all. But then with hindsight, we could all have done it differently.
- *What would you now do differently?* Each question builds on the former. Nowhere in any of this does the coach instruct. The coach may have some tremendous ideas, and may have seen it all before. It is what the individual comes up with independent of the coach that is relevant, and it is what the individual identifies as being the solution that will work.
- *What do you feel about it?* Commitment, determination, attitude—these are all internal emotions. If achievement is about emotions, and passion, and intensity, then it is essential that the coach puts the person being coached in touch with those feelings.

It is more usual to ask:

How do you feel?

It is also usual to answer:

OK

Or

All right.

We are conditioned to say 'OK', or something similar, in the same way that when someone answers:

Well not so good

the natural reaction inside is to say to yourself:

I wish I hadn't asked.

For that reason, we always tend to say: 'OK' when asked:

How are you?

In any case 'How are you', and its derivatives, has in common usage come to be a statement, a greeting, not a question. In the same way as 'OK' has come to be the response, not a fact.

'What are you feeling?' *is* a question, and it makes the person being coached think.

- *Where do you feel it?* Now this may sound a strange enquiry. Nevertheless, it is one of the most powerful questions to ask. Being able to focus on the point inside where either the achievement is felt, or the failure stems, is emphatically cathartic. It brings about 'specific focus'. Putting people in touch with their feelings and pinpointing where those feelings come from is a powerful tool. If an achievement is realized, knowing exactly how that was achieved and where it was felt, assists the person being coached to repeat the process later and can actually accelerate goal achievement. Knowing where the feeling comes from when faced with failure or difficulty allows the person to focus in on the exact point, deal with it, and put it right. Whether the focus is correct in the opinion of the coach is neither here nor there.

For example, in golf, if the coach discerns from observation that the way I, as a novice, am holding my club is hampering my swing, but I determine that the problem is caused by an uncomfortable feeling in my elbow, then the solution is in focusing on the uncomfortable feeling in my elbow, and making it feel comfortable. Eventually, we will most probably get around to dealing with the way in which I am holding the club, but for immediate improvement, whatever the person being coached identifies is correct.

If, as a sales manager, the coach is observing a sales presentation that resulted in failure, and in the debrief the person being coached decides that sitting forward would have improved the performance, but the coach feels that not having asked a single open question was to blame, then sitting forward is correct. If the person being coached felt uncomfortable, then a new sitting position might make him or her feel better, and in so doing, improve the presentation.

Similarly, the repetition of a mistake while using a software program might have more to do with a discomfort caused by the height of a chair, rather than an inability to concentrate. Perhaps the height of the chair causes a lack of concentration. Whatever it is, it is important that it is the person being coached who decides what to do differently. The coach may well have the solution, and can see what the problem is, but verbalizing it without being invited to does not work. You yourself must have several examples of having told someone what the answer was, only to see him or her make the same mistake minutes later. We have all heard the phrase:

I must have told him a thousand times!

Empowering Empowerment is the placing of the responsibility for the performance on the individual. If the coach is also the manager, that does not mean that the manager abdicates responsibility. The manager remains accountable for overall results and the performance of the team. Managers cannot be responsible for individual performance, although many operate on this basis. At the moment of execution of the coaching plan by the individual, it is the person being coached who is responsible.

For empowerment to work, the manager must have absolute trust in the individual employee's capacity to succeed. The employee, in turn, must have trust in the manager, that mistakes will be tolerated. Too many people operate on the basis of not making mistakes, and yet without mistakes people will never experience success. Empowering people means allowing them to find their way. It is the cornerstone of coaching. It shows an ultimate belief in the ability of the employee to achieve. Empowering people means treating them as adults who are capable of making decisions for themselves, especially the routine decisions that clog up most of a normal manager's day.

By creating an empowering environment, work will take on a new meaning for many staff. People want to be involved. If it appears to you that the contrary exists in your company then it probably has more to do with the way in which people are or have been treated in the past. And just because you tried it once and it did not work, do not assume that it will not work in the future. Remember, if you have operated in a certain way for a number of years, then it is unreasonable to expect staff to change just because you change the way you treat them for a fortnight.

The Levi Strauss organization has for a number of years now been in the throes of empowering staff to become involved in the management of their business, and to make most of the daily decisions in their work environment. It has not been easy. Employees have expressed a suspicion about the motives of managers. The Chief Executive, however, said that he would be surprised if they were not suspicious. Treating people one way for a century hardly prepares them well to be treated a totally different way. The employees themselves also admitted that the problems associated with this new way of managing had a lot to do with their own resistance to change. Suddenly many of the work teams were faced with having to sort out poor-performing colleagues, whereas before that was the supervisor's responsibility. The good news is that, even though painful, Levi Strauss continues to move from success to success after once more taking the company into private hands.

Questions to ask: • *So what do you now have to do about it?* At this point the individual could say:

I suppose what you are telling me is . . .

or something similar. Many people have behind them a lifetime of being told what to do, and even at this stage in the process may seek to put the responsibility for potential failure on to the coach. The coach needs to make the individual absolutely aware of whose responsibility it now is to move forward. For example:

I'm not telling you anything at this stage. Whatever you do is up to you. You are responsible for your performance. What is it you now want to do?

Having gained that commitment, it is important to reinforce it:

Is that what you want to do?

- *How much trust do you have in your ability to do it?* At this juncture it becomes important to measure the level of commitment of the person being coached. Is he or she doing it because there is a very real desire for this, or is it due to some external influence, such as the coach? Unless the person being coached is convinced of personal ability and that success is possible, it is likely that failure will ensue. A strong supplementary question now is:
- *On a scale of 1–10, what is the likelihood of your succeeding or of carrying out this task?* If the person being coached identifies the likelihood of success as being a 7 or below, then the chances are that he or she will not succeed, and the process should begin again. The coach may also decide that further investment of time is now questionable. Remember, coaching is not counselling. The coach has aims, and in the case of the coach being a manager, may also have urgent organizational goals to achieve. It is quite in order for the coach, having heard a commitment of less than 7, to say:

I now have a problem in investing more of my time in something which you feel has a less than certain chance of success.

The discussion following this statement can be enlightening. At this stage, the coach and person being coached can revisit the goal, redefine the deadline, or examine why the person being coached appears not totally committed. It could be the wrong goal, that is why the questions are powerful. Too many people invest energy in ill-defined goals, which because they have not been examined in detail often fail to materialize before the journey even begins.

- *What immediate support do you want from me?* The contract is a joint one. The person being coached needs to feel that there is support, and the coach needs to offer it. This is that last chance to get it right before going for the goal.
- *Do it!* The coach empowers the individual to achieve the goal. The instruction is directive. Throughout the whole process, the coach has avoided telling the individual what to do, precisely because the time to tell is now, and it therefore has maximum impact. That is not to say that during the rest of the process the coach may not offer advice.

'Do it' should be the first and only time in the initial stages that the coach tells the individual what to do, and yet, the coach is not really prescribing *what* to do, merely to do *what the person being coached* has identified as the correct course of action.

Review Coaching only works if, following the agreement on a course of action, the coach then observes the individual carrying out the task immediately. One of the biggest problems with the manager as a coach is that managers are prone to agreeing courses of action and then abdicating responsibility by saying:

Come back and see me next week and tell me how you got on.

Staff who know how to play this game come back a week later and say:

I did what you said, and it didn't work!

This process may be the first time that a person has truly committed himself or herself to a specific course of action. As a colleague of mine puts it so well:

By taking that course of action, they run the danger of putting themselves in a position of succeeding.

Strange to say, many people fail because they are frightened of not succeeding, and therefore rarely put themselves in the position of a risk of failure. What they fail to understand is that the points of failure and success cross at the same junction. Succeeding or failing is irrelevant. All that each individual can do is to focus on personal performance, and commit himself or herself to action.

The coach, by immediately offering to observe, again tests the commitment of the individual. It also shows the commitment of the coach to help the individual succeed.

Questions to ask: • *What happened?* Did the person being coached do what he or she promised to do? This discussion cannot take place without the coach having been there to observe what happened. Getting feedback from an individual about what he or she did, and what happened, without first-hand knowledge, is a pointless and fruitless exchange. The coach observes and compares against what was agreed:

What were you trying to do? What did you do? What did you feel? Where did you feel it? What would you do differently?

The process is the same as that which went before. The added advantage is that at this stage, both coach and individual have additional data to hand—experience of the event. It can prove invaluable.

Fulfilment

The end result of implementing the POWER model will be the addition of the letters 'FUL', standing for fulfilment of the goals of the individual, the coach and the organization—POWERFUL. A true sense of achievement comes from fulfilment of our latent talents. So often, well-meaning managers and trainers, faced with employees who appear to be struggling, give them the answers, only to sit by bemused as those, to them, obvious answers are ignored, and the employee fails:

I told her what to do, she just didn't listen.

It's frustrating. I've explained to him a million times how to do it, he just doesn't seem to understand.

In workshops with managers, I regularly elicit that instructions given to employees to work harder, see more people, pay greater attention to detail, continually fail to improve performance. Employees are not in possession of inferior brains, which seem incapable of working out for themselves that working harder, seeing more people, or paying greater attention to detail would improve their performance. Yet managers, faced with performance problems, persistently rely upon the same old panaceas, when in reality the answer invariably lies within the employee. The answer may be the very one proffered by the manager. The difference is that if the employee comes up with the answer, the level of commitment is so high as to make success almost inevitable. Self-fulfilment comes from self-direction and self-control. All are arrived at through self-decision-making. What continually amazes me is that trainers and coaches recognize in themselves the need to arrive at answers themselves, but seem oblivious to the needs in others.

Summary

- The coaching model used is POWER. The word stands for *Purpose, Objectives, What is happening now?, Empowering,* and *Review.*
- Used in sequence it represents a powerful training and management tool for developing and increasing performance in individuals. While logically sequential in nature, many of the elements can be returned to before arriving at the end goal.
- In many cases, lack of performance has more to do with ill-defined goals than a failure to employ both energy and commitment to the task.
- Responsibility for performance lies with the individual.
- Responsibility for support rests with the coach.
- In the case of line managers who act as coach, they may also be accountable ultimately for performance of the individual. However, without employment of the coaching techniques prescribed above they will rarely elicit sustainable high performance from individuals.
- The coach has a responsibility to observe performance in the field immediately after the action plans have been agreed. Failure to do so leaves the coach relying on theoretical feedback, and the individual with an opportunity to delay implementation.
- Table 6.1 can be copied and kept as an *aide mémoire.*

Recommended reading

Alpander, Guvence G. (1991) 'Developing managers' ability to empower employees', *Journal of Management Development,* **10**(3).

Burdett, John O. (1991) 'What is empowerment anyway?', *Journal of European Industrial Training,* **15**(6).

Ripley, Robert E. and Marie J. (1992) 'Empowerment, the cornerstone of quality', *Management Decision,* **30**(4).

Smiles, Samuel (1986) *Self Help.* Penguin.

Stewart, Douglas (1986) *The Power of People Skills.* John Wiley and Sons, Inc.

Table 6.1 *Power coaching—the model, and accompanying questions to ask*

Purpose
- How much time have we got?
- What is the purpose of this session for you?
- What are you looking for from me?

Objectives
- What are you trying to achieve?
- Is this your goal, or someone else's?
- (How can you make it your goal?)
- Is this the whole goal, or is it part of something more long term that you want to achieve?
- What will you feel like when you achieve your goal?
- (Can you see yourself achieving your goal?)
- Is there anything else that you could do?
- Which course of action do you favour and why?
- When do you want to achieve this goal by?
- How realistic is that?

What is happening now?
- What have you done about it so far?
- What was the result?
- What have been the obstacles?
- How did you set about overcoming them?
- What would you now do differently?
- What do you feel about it?
- Where do you feel it?

Empowering
- So what do you now have to do about it?
- How much trust do you have in your ability to do it?
- On a scale of 1–10, what is the likelihood of your succeeding?
- What immediate support do you want from me?
- Do it!

Review
- What happened?
- What were you trying to do?
(return to the beginning of the model)

---

7 How good a coach are you?

One of the best ways to help managers understand where they are in terms of coaching skills is to get them to complete a self-questionnaire. You can either use your own or adopt the one contained in this chapter. Are they scientific? No. But that is not the point. On any training course, and especially on management training courses, most people are there for purely selfish reasons. If you can give them something which is unique to them, it helps both the learning process and also the acceptance of the training event. Most self-completed questionnaires I have used and seen, and that includes the majority of those that are supposed to be scientific instruments, fall far short of being of any use whatsoever, other than as entertainment value. There is absolutely nothing wrong with being entertaining on a training course. The effect of saying to a manager, or anybody else for that matter:

I will now be getting you to complete a questionnaire, from which we will be able to draw your own personal profile. This profile will be unique to you, and will help you to determine your coaching style, identify areas of strength, and highlight for you areas that you need to develop

will ensure complete candidate attention and participation. Your reputation will be further enhanced when you feed them back the result. Everybody believes everything a self-questionnaire tells them. You see, candidates are asked to answer a series of questions about themselves. They are then fed back the answers. Remarkably the answers match what they think about themselves. Astounding! If you can organize to administer the inventory on a computer, so much the better. People believe anything a computer comes out with.

A coaching style inventory

A number of coaching situations are given below. After each situation is outlined, a choice of three alternative reactions is suggested. You must rank the alternatives in order, where '1' is your first choice, '2' is your second choice, and '3' is your third choice.

Situation 1

> The person you are coaching has under-performed for some considerable time. You have been unable to spend any time with her due to pressure of work elsewhere, but at last have arranged to allocate a day's coaching with her. This is the start of the session.

Your initial reaction

Item	Alternatives	Ranking
1.1	'There's a problem here with your perform-ance and I'm here today to help you resolve that, and together I'm sure we will succeed.'	
1.2	'We seem to have a problem here with your performance—what do you think is the answer?'	
1.3	'I see my job today as helping you to perform better, no matter where the starting point is. What do you expect of me today?'	

Situation 2

You have asked one of your staff to come into your office to see you. The purpose for you is to arrange a coaching session with him. His performance has not been good in the near past.

Your initial reaction

Item	Alternatives	Ranking
2.1	'I want you to arrange to show me how you do your job so that I can help you improve your performance. When would be the best time?'	
2.2	'My intention is to accompany you on the job regularly so that we can improve your overall performance. I'd like to come out with you tomorrow.'	
2.3	'So, why do you think I've asked to see you?'	

Situation 3

You have identified a situation in which a member of your team is performing badly. The individual concerned comes up with an idea to improve performance.

Your initial reaction

Item	Alternatives	Ranking
3.1	'That's a good idea. Do you think there is any downside to it?'	
3.2	'Well it looks all right on the surface, but I think you may have a problem implementing it.'	
3.3	'That's good. Is there anything else you could do?'	

Situation 4

> Following a coaching session, you have agreed a course of action with the individual member of staff. You now want to implement it.

Your initial reaction

Item	Alternatives	Ranking
4.1	'When do you propose to put this plan into action?'	
4.2	'What I suggest is that you try this out and come back to me within seven days and tell me how you got on.'	
4.3	'I now need to watch you implement this plan, when are you going to do it?'	

Situation 5

> The member of staff has steadfastly been unable to identify any personal improvement plan. According to him, he is trying as hard as he can.

Your initial reaction

Item	Alternatives	Ranking
5.1	'What exactly is it that you want to do?'	
5.2	'What have you done so far, and what effect has that had?'	
5.3	'It looks as though you might not be suitable for this job.'	

Situation 6

> During the initial coaching discussion you know that the individual is looking at the wrong problem.

Your initial reaction

Item	Alternatives	Ranking
6.1	'It seems to me that you are looking at the wrong area.'	
6.2	'Do you want my opinion as to what the real problem might be?'	
6.3	'On a scale of 1–10, what is the likelihood of that course of action working?'	

Situation 7	The individual has tried to implement the agreed plan, but there has been no improvement in performance.

Your initial reaction

Item	Alternatives	Ranking
7.1	'What exactly did we agree, what did you do, and what happened?'	
7.2	'OK, so that didn't work, what else could we do?'	
7.3	'Perhaps you didn't try hard enough.'	

Situation 8	Just before meeting the member of staff you were given some information from someone else which highlighted the performance problem as being a personal situation at home.

Your initial reaction

Item	Alternatives	Ranking
8.1	'I seem to sense that perhaps there's something wrong at home.'	
8.2	'Is there something troubling you that you haven't told me about?'	
8.3	What's happening for you at the moment?'	

Situation 9	This is now the sixth time you have met and on each occasion the individual has failed to implement agreed action plans.

Your initial reaction

Item	Alternatives	Ranking
9.1	'For this relationship to work, you have to keep your part of the bargain.'	
9.2	'Why haven't you done what you said you would?'	
9.3	'I've tried my best to help, but it is a hopeless case.'	

Situation 10

> The individual seems incapable of implementing what has been discussed. The only alternative is for you to show him how to do it.

Your initial reaction

Item	Alternatives	Ranking
10.1	'Look, I'll show you how to do it.'	
10.2	'Do you want me to show you how to do it?'	
10.3	'Where do you feel the main difficulty is in implementing this action?'	

Situation 11

> When you asked the individual whether she had any more ideas, she said she could not think of any.

Your initial reaction

Item	Alternatives	Ranking
11.1	'I have some ideas that might help, but it is up to you if you want to hear them.'	
11.2	'So what do we do now?'	
11.3	'Come on. Try again.'	

Situation 12

> When you asked the individual to say what he wanted to do, he said 'Anything you want—you're the boss.'

Your initial reaction

Item	Alternatives	Ranking
12.1	'I want you to start doing your job, that's what I want.'	
12.2	'What do you want?'	
12.3	'What do you think I want?'	

Situation 13

> Your boss asks you why it is taking so long to improve your member of staff's performance. You have the feeling it will never improve.

	Item	Alternatives	Ranking
Your initial reaction	13.1	'I have the feeling it's never going to get better.'	
	13.2	'It's up to him. We just have to be patient.'	
	13.3	'He's now had long enough. I'm thinking about asking him to leave. What's your opinion?'	

Situation 14 — Your member of staff has tried very hard to implement the plan, but he does not seem to be moving forward. He says 'It's impossible, I might as well throw in the towel.'

	Item	Alternatives	Ranking
Your initial reaction	14.1	'What effect will that have on you?'	
	14.2	'That's quitting. I thought you were made of stronger stuff.'	
	14.3	'Well, that's up to you.'	

Situation 15 — During a particularly bad coaching session, the individual tells you that the reason he cannot perform to standard is that there are very difficult situations at home which he cannot get off his mind.

	Item	Alternatives	Ranking
Your initial reaction	15.1	'What do you want to do now?'	
	15.2	'We've all got problems. The important thing is not to let it affect your work.'	
	15.3	'I think the best thing is for you to go home and sort it out.'	

Situation 16 — The individual is having difficulty implementing any performance improvement. She says 'Look, every time I have a problem you ask me a question. You're the manager, just tell me what to do.'

Your initial reaction	*Item*	*Alternatives*	*Ranking*
	16.1	'What do you prefer, me always telling you what to do, or you finding out for yourself?'	
	16.2	'If I keep coming up with the answer, and it keeps not working, where do you think that leaves me?'	
	16.3	'All right, I want you to get moving and do what you're paid to do.'	

Situation 17 When you ask the individual what the goal is, she says 'I have to reach target don't I?'

Your initial reaction	*Item*	*Alternatives*	*Ranking*
	17.1	'That's up to you isn't it?'	
	17.2	'Not really. It's what you have to do, but sometimes it might not be your personal goal.'	
	17.3	'Is reaching the target your goal?'	

Situation 18 You ask the individual what help he wants. He cannot think of any.

Your initial reaction	*Item*	*Alternatives*	*Ranking*
	18.1	'What about me coming out with you?'	
	18.2	'Does that mean you can perform to standard without help?'	
	18.3	'If you want, I can make some suggestions.'	

Situation 19

> The individual says all the right things, but you still feel uneasy, and her performance never improves.

Your initial reaction

Item	Alternatives	Ranking
19.1	'I have to say that I feel uncomfortable with your behaviour. You say the right things, however, you don't appear to implement any plans we agree.'	
19.2	'I don't believe you.'	
19.3	'If you are doing all the right things, why is it that your performance never improves?'	

Situation 20

> This is now the last chance. Your boss has given you a deadline either to improve the individual's performance or to get rid of him. During the coaching session, the individual says he will take a particular course of action. In the past he has never kept to any previous commitment.

Your initial reaction

Item	Alternatives	Ranking
20.1	'Look, this is the last chance. If you don't get it right this time you're out.'	
20.2	'What has happened in the past when we have agreed this course of action?'	
20.3	'I am under pressure from my boss to get rid of you, so it better work this time.'	

Score Sheet

Put your ranking against the item number.

Item	Rank	Item	Rank	Item	Rank
1.3		1.1		1.2	
2.1		2.2		2.3	
3.3		3.1		3.2	
4.3		4.1		4.2	
5.1		5.2		5.3	
6.1		6.2		6.3	
7.1		7.2		7.3	
8.3		8.2		8.1	
9.1		9.2		9.3	
10.3		10.2		10.1	
11.1		11.3		11.2	
12.2		12.3		12.1	
13.3		13.1		13.2	
14.1		14.3		14.2	
15.1		15.3		15.2	
16.1		16.2		16.3	
17.3		17.1		17.2	
18.3		18.2		18.1	
19.1		19.3		19.2	
20.2		20.1		20.3	
Total 'A'		Total 'B'		Total 'C'	

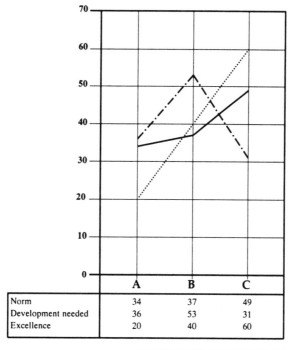

	A	B	C
Norm	34	37	49
Development needed	36	53	31
Excellence	20	40	60

KEY:

———————	Norm
—·—·—	Development needed
············	Excellence

Figure 7.1 *Coaching profiles*

Feedback I found that the average profile (shown in Figure 7.1) was a score of 34 in 'A', 37 in 'B', and 49 in 'C'. In fact, if you have a score of between 31 and 40 in column 'A' I would say that you have a good grasp of coaching principles and the model. A score of between 20 and 30 in 'A' would show a remarkable theoretical ability. I say theoretical, because as in all things to do with skills acquisition the proof of the pudding is in the application. If your score in 'A' is between 41 and 60, then you still have some way to go. You need to consider how much you stick to being in control, and whether you are yet able to empower people— keep with it.

8 The coach in action

This chapter focuses on a number of examples taken from actual case studies in which the coaching model has been used. I have changed the names of the players, but the situations are real enough. I will show how coaching has enhanced performance in a number of roles. Also explained will be the coaching role of the trainer in terms of his or her relationship with managers, defined as a metacoach.

Case study 8.1

Learning to use a spreadsheet

Nearly all forms of computer systems training leave trainees bemused, and trainers frustrated. Within an hour most trainees are totally confused and trainers are usually oblivious to the lights having gone out. Over the last seven years I have evaluated numerous computer training events across a multitude of companies and individual events, and can guarantee that current practices in computer systems training for initial non-users are a total waste of time and money. The problem most trainers are faced with is that computer systems change so rapidly, and therefore the tendency is to employ external agents to carry out training. It is not uncommon to find that these trainers while vaguely competent in the software package, are usually the worst of trainers. In addition, the way in which they work demands that training sessions are most likely to be a full day minimum. I am sure that if you examine the success of these events you will find that most people learn little after the first hour.

Before moving on to coaching in computer systems I strongly recommend that you adopt some basic rules for computer training:

Rule 1   *Each training event should last no more than one hour.* As I have said, for most people, more than one hour's computer training produces something akin to brain-death.

Rule 2   *The first event should not proceed until the trainer has drawn up plans to test understanding and competence after each hour.* I have found that if trainers were to test for Rule 2 after each hour has passed they would be amazed at how little has sunk in. Instead of which most computer systems trainers drone on for hours, oblivious to an increasingly comatose audience.

The coach cannot begin coaching until trainees have reached a level of basic competence, but then having done so, the effect can be dramatic in reinforcing and embedding learning.

Rule 3   The coach should resist telling the trainee what to do.

In this case study the trainee had received some training but was not progressing very well and the manager was concerned that perhaps the individual was not suited to operating computer-based systems.

COACH   The first thing we need to agree is the purpose of this first meeting.
TRAINEE   Well it is to learn to use the spreadsheet.
COACH   Is it to learn to use the spreadsheet or is it about deciding how to go about learning to use it?
TRAINEE   My boss says I have to learn about it.
COACH   How long has he given you?
TRAINEE   He just says that he needs me to use this new spreadsheet as soon as possible.
COACH   And what is the reason for that?
TRAINEE   The new budgetary controls and forecasts all work on this.
COACH   And what would be the effect of your becoming competent in using the system?

For the sake of brevity I have cut down the length of this introduction, but some of these initial discussions can be tortuous. The reason being that in most cases people do not volunteer to undertake new systems training. Generally they are told that a new system is being introduced and that they have to learn it. I have conducted field trials on the traditional method of learning and compared it to the coaching style. In each case, people learnt more rapidly, were more competent, and output of work was of a higher quality and quantity using the coaching model. In this particular case, as in so many others, training can often be seen as an intrusion, something which trainees are forced to undertake, and therefore their acceptance and learning are impaired. What I was looking to do here was to make the trainee find a personal benefit which could be moulded into a personal goal.

TRAINEE   It would get him off my back for one thing.
COACH   And would that be of benefit?
TRAINEE   It certainly would. He's a bit of a tyrant if we don't get things right.
COACH   So what will you feel like when you can demonstrate to him your competence?
TRAINEE   I'll feel a lot better. I don't seem to be getting to grips with it at all.
COACH   So John, the purpose then of this meeting is to prepare a plan which will enable you to competently use the spreadsheet within four weeks so that you can help your boss to produce the budgetary forecasts for the finance department each month end.
TRAINEE   Yes, that sounds good, when do I start?
COACH   Well, first thing we need to agree is whether that is possible, and what my role is.
TRAINEE   I suppose it's possible. Other people are doing it, and your role is to teach me.
COACH   Well, perhaps, we should set a goal of finding out whether it is possible by reviewing progress at the end of this session. So far as my role as teacher

is concerned, you've had teaching before, and yet it doesn't seem to have sunk in. Is that fair?

TRAINEE   Yes, I suppose so. Maybe the last trainer wasn't very good.

COACH   That could very well be the case. What else could have been the problem?

TRAINEE   I suppose you want me to say that I wasn't a very good pupil.

COACH   I don't want to say anything that you don't want to. All I am interested in is to examine a range of alternative reasons and possible options for a solution.

TRAINEE   OK. It might have been me.

COACH   Anything else?

TRAINEE   I don't think so.

COACH   I've thought of something which might have contributed if you are interested in exploring it.

TRAINEE   Yes, what is it?

COACH   What about the way in which your training was arranged. Were you comfortable with it?

TRAINEE   Well not really. It all happened a bit too quickly. There was too much to take in and by the end of the day I was totally confused.

COACH   So what could we do that would make you feel more comfortable?

TRAINEE   Take it slower, and let me practise each part of the system until I get it right before going on.

COACH   Are there any problems with that?

TRAINEE   It will take a long time.

COACH   So what are the benefits?

TRAINEE   At least I won't forget it.

COACH   And what will you feel about doing it right?

TRAINEE   I'll feel more confident.

COACH   And how do you think you will approach the next lesson?

TRAINEE   I'll probably be better at it, and might even do it quicker.

COACH   So what else could you do to speed it up?

TRAINEE   I could practise more often.

COACH   And when could you do that?

TRAINEE   Whenever I get the chance during the day.

COACH   Anything else?

TRAINEE   Well I suppose I could stay back for a while and practise after work.

COACH   Is that what you want to do?

TRAINEE   Not really.

COACH   So what will be the effect of not practising?

TRAINEE   I'll be no further forward.

COACH   What have you actually done about it so far?

TRAINEE   You mean about learning to use it? Not a lot.

COACH   And the result of that?

TRAINEE   I've got no better at it.

COACH   What were the obstacles?

TRAINEE   Nothing really, just me. I didn't see why I had to practise in my own time for something I didn't bring into the department.

COACH   And now?

TRAINEE   I can see there's something in it for me.

COACH   And what do you feel about it?

TRAINEE   I'm ready to give it a go.

Although it may seem a long process, the benefit here for me was that I now had a trainee with a totally different attitude towards learning, and the battle appeared almost won without even touching the keyboard. As in all things concerned with performance enhancement, the key is in the mind.

COACH   Now, please put the spreadsheet up on the screen. You've told me that this is as far as you reached last time before things started going wrong.

TRAINEE   Well the trainer ran through some of the buttons I had to press but I forgot which ones. I have to keep switching the thing off to get back to the start.

COACH   What is it you want to do?

TRAINEE   I want to prepare a forecast for the month's sales.

COACH   How do you think you might do that?

TRAINEE   I suppose I type the figures in that column.

COACH   How will you know which month they relate to?

TRAINEE   I need to have the months at the top of the columns.

COACH   Then do it.

The trainee typed in the words, putting spaces between the months. However, as he did not 'tab' between columns, the words gathered together in one column, and eventually as the column width was used up, disappeared.

COACH   So what's happening?

TRAINEE   I don't know. The words are at the bottom of the screen but they don't appear in the column.

COACH   What is it you want to do?

TRAINEE   I want to put a separate month in each column.

COACH   How were you trying to move from column to column?

TRAINEE   I pressed the space bar.

COACH   And what happened?

TRAINEE   It just put a space into the column.

COACH   Which other key could you press to jump to the next column?

TRAINEE   The 'tab'?

COACH   Do it then and let's see what happens.

TRAINEE   The cursor moved to the next column.

COACH   So what will you do next time when you want to move between columns?

TRAINEE   I'll press the 'tab' key.

COACH   What do you want to do next?

As we progressed, the trainee learnt more in 20 minutes than he had learnt in days. In reality, he had learnt how to use the spreadsheet, but was unable to apply that learning. This is a very simple example of part of a coaching process that taught someone to learn how to use a spreadsheet in a fraction of the time taken by traditional learning methods. For any coach using this method, it may appear very slow over the first few lessons but it will become evident that the trainee retains far more information and becomes more competent quickly. In this particular case, John managed to become an accomplished user of a number of systems, eventually training others to use computer systems. As we progressed, I was able to coach John in systems with which, while not a complete beginner, I had little expertise myself.

Case study 8.2

Gaining sales appoint-
ments by telephone

Sheila was a trainee life insurance salesperson. She recently attended a sales course where she was taught to use a particular sales script that had been found to be effective. When she started in the field, her appointment rate was very poor, which was put down to her inability to get client appointments by telephone. She was now in danger of not surviving her probationary period. As in the previous case study we had covered the purpose of the session, and what I felt I was able to achieve within the time-scale.

COACH   What's the long-term goal from contacting people?
TRAINEE   To sell them some life assurance.
COACH   What will stop that from happening?
TRAINEE   Well for a start they might not want to see me.
COACH   Does that happen often?
TRAINEE   Quite a lot.
COACH   Why is that?
TRAINEE   I don't know. They just don't want insurance.
COACH   Is that what you're asking for?
TRAINEE   No. I ask for an appointment to see them.
COACH   So it's the appointment they turn down is it?
TRAINEE   I suppose so.
COACH   Before we progress, you need to decide what it is that they are objecting to.
TRAINEE   I don't know.
COACH   Are you using the telephone sales script you were given?
TRAINEE   Yes.
COACH   Say it to me.

The trainee repeated her version of the script, which as it turned out was not the same one she had been supplied with.

COACH   It's not the same as the one we developed last time.
TRAINEE   It didn't work.
COACH   How often did it not work?
TRAINEE   I don't know. I tried it a few times and it didn't work.
COACH   So you changed it.
TRAINEE   Yes.
COACH   And what happened?
TRAINEE   It still doesn't work.
COACH   What do you think the reason is?
TRAINEE   They still don't want insurance.
COACH   Can we go back to the beginning? What is it you want from me?

In some cases trainees can be hostile to change and any implied criticism. It can be frustrating for the coach sometimes to be faced with someone who appears to lack any positive intention of learning, but the coach needs to focus at this stage, not on the reticence of the trainee but on his or her own coaching performance. I pursued the point.

TRAINEE   Well. I'm not getting any appointments. I think it's more to do with the fact the business is tight at the moment, rather than my style. I've done what you said, but it doesn't work.

COACH   Just a minute. At the moment, the script you developed does not work. Others using the same script are making it work. Let me hear you say the script we gave you.

The trainee repeated her own version. I asked her to say it again three more times.

COACH   It's different every time.
TRAINEE   Well it's flexible. It depends on what the prospect says.
COACH   Yet not only am I the same person listening, but I also haven't said anything yet.

It took some time but the trainee eventually realized that she did not have a script and the request for the appointment depended entirely on how she felt at the time. Considering that getting appointments by telephone is most salespeople's *bête noire*, she usually felt very negative and nervous about making telephone calls—hence the poor reponse.

COACH   I want you to use the script.

There are times when the coach has to impose a regime. It is pointless allowing people to run the 100 m in whatever direction they like—they would be disqualified. When you coach a football team there are rules about the area of play and the time allowed each half. In some sales situations, and this is the part most salespeople and managers resist, there may be rules, like a script, which have to be enforced. I had already proven, by using this particular scripting method, that the appointment rates for other salespeople had increased dramatically. In some cases it had helped to move people from a 20 per cent strike rate to 80 per cent within one session. If, as a coach, you have prescribed something which works as part of the initial training programme, which was the case here, and people who choose to ignore it have not found a better regime, which again was the situation here, before going on the coach can insist on imposing what was agreed at the training stage.

COACH   I want to use the script and I am going to watch you, listen to you and record your performance.

In this scenario it was shown to the trainee that her performance was so poor that even those wanting to buy insurance would not give her an appointment. I insisted she keep practising the same script, playing it back to her each time. Each time it sounded better. Within an hour of adopting the script and having her performance coached, she was achieving high levels of success on the telephone.

Case study 8.3

Training the trainer   Peter was a training consultant, writing and delivering training events to all levels of staff. While an accomplished writer, his delivery style was very stilted, so much so that the response he used to get from course delegates was less than favourable. I watched his presentations on a number of occasions and although I found them to be technically accomplished, they lacked something. I noticed that Peter wrote all of his notes out in minute detail prior to delivering a session. During a session he would have his notes in front of him, meticulously typed up and laid out so that he could see them. As soon as he moved away from his notes, however, he looked and sounded ill at ease.

I remember some time ago, before I adopted a coaching style myself, telling him to forget his notes and deliver from slides. It is the style I utilize. I put my slides together first, then write up a script, and then deliver from the slides. The advice had gone unheeded. I gauged that saying to him:

I told you so

would not be helpful!

COACH   Peter I've got 30 minutes now. How can we best utilize the time?
PETER   I'd like you to help me sort out this problem with my delivery. I just can't get it right.
COACH   In 30 minutes Peter it might not be possible to do a complete job. Can I suggest that you present your latest session to me. I'll watch it, and record it. We can have a brief discussion, after which I want you to watch the video playback, and tell me what you see.

Peter agreed. I arranged for a couple of people to attend the session. His presentation took 15 minutes, and sure enough, during it, while he stayed near his notes everything went well. As soon as he ventured out of sight of his notes it became lack-lustre. The problem was also, that even when in sight of his notes, because he kept looking down, the whole presentation lacked impact. After the others had left, we discussed it.

COACH   What did you feel?
TRAINEE   I don't know. It was all right, but it wasn't great.
COACH   What were you trying to do?
TRAINEE   I was attempting to impart some knowledge.
COACH   Anything else?
TRAINEE   I suppose I was trying to motivate people to learn.
COACH   Did you achieve that?
TRAINEE   I don't think so.
COACH   How do you know?
TRAINEE   I didn't feel good, and they didn't look particularly inspired.

I had been rewinding the tape, and began playing it back with the volume switched off.

COACH   Where didn't you feel comfortable?
TRAINEE   What do you mean?
COACH   You say you didn't feel good. By that do you mean comfortable?
TRAINEE   Yes.
COACH   So where wasn't it comfortable?
TRAINEE   I don't know. Do you mean physically?
COACH   Yes.
TRAINEE   I suppose round about here.

He pointed to his shoulder.

COACH   Look at the playback, and tell me what's happening.

A video can be a very useful tool, especially if used correctly. I find it extremely useful to turn the sound off on playback, as the noise can be distracting. In most cases what you want to focus on are the body movements. In a case like this, they tell you a lot more about performance than the words do.

TRAINEE   I don't look too happy.
COACH   What else?
TRAINEE   I look uncomfortable.
COACH   All the time?
TRAINEE   No, just some of the time.
COACH   When in particular?
TRAINEE   When I am standing near the desk. And when I return to my desk.
COACH   What about when you move away from the desk?
TRAINEE   It looks all right.
COACH   So what is there about the desk?
TRAINEE   It's where the overhead projector is.
COACH   How do you look when you are changing the slides.
TRAINEE   OK.
COACH   So what else is there on the desk?
TRAINEE   My notes are on it.

Peter began to laugh.

COACH   What are you laughing at?
TRAINEE   You're going to tell me it's the notes, you've told me that before.
COACH   I'm not going to tell you anything. What do you do when you stand at the desk and when you return to the desk?
TRAINEE   I look at my notes.
COACH   And what happens?
TRAINEE   I look unhappy. But I'm not you see. I'm only studying my notes.
COACH   I understand. But what do you look like?
TRAINEE   Unhappy.
COACH   And what effect is it having on the audience?
TRAINEE   It makes them unhappy.
COACH   So what else could you do?
TRAINEE   I could smile.
COACH   What else?
TRAINEE   I could look at them more.
COACH   What will that mean?
TRAINEE   I won't be able to do both. I mean I can't look at them and my notes.
COACH   What else could you do?
TRAINEE   I could learn my notes. But I might forget something.
COACH   Will they know?
TRAINEE   I don't suppose so.
COACH   When do you look happy?
TRAINEE   When I'm standing in the front of the table. Except for that part.
COACH   What happened there?
TRAINEE   I forgot about something and went back to the table to look at my notes.
COACH   If you're interested I could suggest another way of looking at it, but it's up to you if you want to explore it.
TRAINEE   Yes.

COACH   Could it be, that you didn't forget something as much as remembered that your notes were on the table?

Peter began to laugh again.

COACH   So what do you want to do?
TRAINEE   I want to try it again without my notes.
COACH   When?
TRAINEE   Now.

I asked Peter to do his presentation again a few more times. I left him to record himself, playing it back each time and looking at his performance. I had run out of time, but we did agree that later on I would watch him again. By then he had improved immensely. He is now a very accomplished speaker and continues to improve.

Case study 8.4

Using the coaching model as a performance appraisal tool

Using the POWER model is not restricted to performance improvement in a skills sense. It can be used for interviewing and for appraisals. This is how I used it for the latter.

Margaret was a clerical assistant. Her last boss told me that she just came to work to socialize, and showed little aspiration for doing anything else. I had not spent too much time with Margaret apart from when I took over the department two months previously. Her work appeared to be reasonable, but I had the feeling that she could do a lot better.

COACH   Margaret. Tell me what you want out of this discussion?
TRAINEE   It's the yearly appraisal isn't it?
COACH   That could be my purpose, but what's in it for you?
TRAINEE   If I get a good appraisal, I get a bigger rise.
COACH   What else do you want?
TRAINEE   I'd like to know what you expect of me—what I am supposed to do to get on.
COACH   What are you keen to do?
TRAINEE   Well I don't want to stay a clerical assistant for ever.
COACH   So what do you want from me?
TRAINEE   I suppose I want you to tell me how I get up the ladder.
COACH   So what do you have to do to get promoted?
TRAINEE   Be in the right place at the right time.
COACH   Anything else?
TRAINEE   Do a good job.
COACH   Is that what you want?
TRAINEE   How do you mean? Do a good job, or get promoted?
COACH   Both.
TRAINEE   I suppose they both go together.
COACH   Do they go together as far as you're concerned, or is that the way it works around here?
TRAINEE   That's difficult. I've seen people do a good job and not get promoted, and I've seen some people who don't do a good job but get promoted.

COACH   So which is it for you?

TRAINEE   I'd like to do both.

COACH   So is this a long-term goal of yours, promotion, or is it part of a greater plan?

TRAINEE   I'd like to think I could manage the department at some time. It might not sound likely, but I think I'm capable.

COACH   What's not so likely about it?

TRAINEE   Well it doesn't depend on me does it?

COACH   Who does it depend on then?

TRAINEE   Well people like you for a start.

COACH   So what would make people like me consider you for promotion?

TRAINEE   If I did a good job?

COACH   Anything else?

TRAINEE   I don't know.

COACH   What about making people like me aware about your management aspirations?

TRAINEE   What do you mean?

COACH   I notice from your file that there's no mention of management aspirations.

TRAINEE   I didn't mention it before.

COACH   And what do you feel was the consequence of that?

TRAINEE   Perhaps people thought I wasn't interested.

COACH   So what could you do differently?

TRAINEE   Talk about it.

COACH   Anything else?

TRAINEE   Ask for help.

COACH   In what way?

TRAINEE   Well what do I have to do?

COACH   Can I just check something out first. Is it management you want, just promotion, or is there something else?

TRAINEE   I don't really know. I don't want to be doing this job forever.

COACH   So is it not wanting to be in this job forever, or the fact that you want to manage other people?

TRAINEE   Not particularly, but it seems that it's the only way to get on.

COACH   What do you mean by getting on? What is there about getting on that appeals to you?

TRAINEE   Well I want to feel useful, looked up to, recognized for doing something worth while, something important.

I have observed a great many appraisals over the years. Most are part of the endless paper chase that goes on in organizations, and most eventually lead to arranging for mindless training sessions which simply fill out the requirement that managers have to satisfy agreed training needs at the yearly appraisal. Thousands of people across the country are on management development programmes as a result of poorly conducted appraisals, where it is assumed that everybody and his brother wants to be in management. People simply want to get through the appraisal interview. The answer to most appraisals is usually whatever the training course prospectus contains. I once included an assertiveness training module into a course prospectus for VDU operators just to see what would happen. After the appraisals had been conducted, I had a 97 per cent take-up for assertiveness training. The subject had never come up on a previous appraisal. I could not work out why VDU operators wanted assertiveness training, other than to get away from the VDU perhaps. I cancelled the module and nobody complained, perhaps they did need assertiveness training after all.

I am convinced that if, around the time of appraisals, a training prospectus contained 'Abseiling from the Third Floor', somebody would identify it as a training need.

COACH   Margaret. Is there anything else that you could do apart from management?

TRAINEE   Well I thought about computer programming, but I can't do it.

COACH   What do you mean you can't do it?

TRAINEE   I don't know of anybody who got promoted internally to be a computer programmer. They get them all from the outside.

COACH   Is that what you want to do?

TRAINEE   I'm interested in computers. All I seem to do here though is word-processing.

COACH   So what have you done about it before now?

TRAINEE   Nothing.

COACH   And what was the result?

TRAINEE   Nothing.

COACH   So what could you do?

TRAINEE   Do something about it.

COACH   Such as what?

TRAINEE   I don't know.

COACH   First thing is to decide why you want to do it, then we can work out what to do. Why do it?

TRAINEE   It's something I'm really interested in.

COACH   What is there about it?

TRAINEE   Well I know Carol in Computer Programming, and she really seems to enjoy her job.

COACH   So is it enjoying your job that's important, or having aspirations to be a computer programmer?

TRAINEE   That's difficult. It's just that her job looks more interesting than mine. It looks more complicated, and pays more.

COACH   Is it the complexity of the job that interests you, or the higher pay?

TRAINEE   It probably goes back to what I was saying before, about being recognized, feeling valued.

COACH   Do you feel valued now?

TRAINEE   No, not really.

COACH   What's the problem?

TRAINEE   Well, every day just seems the same. I don't seem to be getting anywhere.

COACH   So what could you do about it?

TRAINEE   I could change jobs.

COACH   Yes, we've looked at that. What else could you do?

TRAINEE   I don't know.

COACH   What about changing this job?

TRAINEE   What do you mean?

COACH   What could you do about the content of this job, that would make it more challenging?

TRAINEE   I've never really thought about it.

COACH   Surely there's something about it, or the department that you've thought you could do better, or change.

TRAINEE   Well we don't appear to be able to provide managers with the answers they want, without a real panic going on. It takes ages and everybody gets a bit distraught with the pressure when there's a rush on to provide some information for the month-end returns.

COACH   So what could you do about it?

TRAINEE   Nothing really. We haven't got the information easily accessible.

COACH   What would make it accessible?

TRAINEE   A computer database for a start, but we haven't got one.

COACH   Do you think it's a good idea?

TRAINEE   Yes I do.

COACH   So what could you do about it?

TRAINEE   Well I could find out about one.

COACH   Is that what you want to do?

TRAINEE   I wouldn't mind. It would be quite interesting.

COACH   What obstacles do you see in the way?

TRAINEE   Cost probably.

COACH   So what could you do about it?

TRAINEE   Prove it was saving money.

COACH   How confident do you feel about doing it then?

TRAINEE   Pretty good. I think I'd like to have a go.

COACH   What else would this project do for you?

TRAINEE   It might give me an insight into computers a bit more.

COACH   And management?

TRAINEE   Yes, it probably would.

COACH   What support do you want from me?

TRAINEE   Well I'd need some help on where to start, and perhaps you could tell me how much we've got in the budget so that I know how far to go.

COACH   Do it then.

Margaret successfully investigated a database for the statistics we needed for the month-end reports. She enjoyed it so much that she went on to implement a number of improvements to the department, part of which was to train other people in adopting the new systems. She didn't become a computer programmer—but became a computer trainer instead. She tells me she loves the freedom of the job, and the last thing she wants is to be a manager.

Case study 8.5

Coaching managers—
the role of the
metacoach

The 'metacoach' is the coach of the coach. Even the coach needs feedback, and similarly the POWER model can be used to give that internal feedback on the coach's performance. The problem you may face with managers is their reluctance to be coached at coaching. A good way to set this up is to arrange a session which involves a physical activity so that all concerned can 'feel' the effect of being coached, and of being coached as a coach.

One way I found that works is either to take managers to a golf driving range, arrange for a golf session indoors using a net, or buy some of those small plastic balls, the size of golf balls, which are hollow and have holes in the sides. These can still be hit quite hard, but they do not inflict any damage when they hit anything. Obviously if you are going to do this indoors, you will need a large room with enough height to be able to swing a golf club. Place a screen 5 to 10 metres away, or hang a large sheet from the ceiling. No matter how hard you hit the ball, the sheet or the screen will stop the ball.

Pick someone who has tried playing golf but is not very good, and find an experienced player to coach him. Explain to the coach that you want him to coach the trainee to hit the ball better. You then stand near the coach, and when appropriate call 'time-out' so that you can ask the coach the same coaching questions that are part of the model. The chances are, for experienced golfers, they will not be able to resist 'telling' people what to do. The effect of your asking the POWER questions will help them realize what it is like to be coached, and what they are doing to the trainee.

If the golf set-up is inappropriate, the same exercise can be achieved through playing snooker. By removing the red balls, leaving only the cue ball and the colours on the table, coaching sessions and metacoaching sessions can be arranged. It is possible to go even further by standing another coach next to the metacoach, asking them what they are trying to achieve. Dependent upon the number of managers available, the metacoach role can be extended infinitively, and at times can result in both an enjoyable, humorous, yet powerful learning experience.

The following case study involves Alex who was a sales manager. He had been on a sales call with Sally. After the call, Alex attempted to coach her to increase her performance next time. I was observing the coaching session and had made some notes, using the suggested feedback form included in Appendix 3. I also find it useful to get the coach to write down the benefits of the coaching session as included in the last section of the form in Appendix 3. You may want to adapt this for everybody being coached.

COACH   What were you trying to achieve Alex?
MANAGER   I was trying to get Sally to admit that she could have performed better on that last call.
COACH   Was that your purpose or hers?
MANAGER   Mine.
COACH   So what was her purpose?
MANAGER   I don't know.
COACH   So what's the problem?
MANAGER   She won't be committed to a course of action if she isn't involved in setting the objectives.
COACH   Good. What about you? What's the purpose of this session?
MANAGER   To help make me a better coach.
COACH   Is that your objective or mine?
MANAGER   Both I suppose.
COACH   What will be the effect of making you a better coach?
MANAGER   The theory is that my people will perform better.
COACH   Is it theory or reality?

MANAGER   At the moment it's theory.

COACH   What's the difference with reality?

MANAGER   Well up to now it hasn't worked.

COACH   What hasn't?

MANAGER   This coaching thing.

COACH   What specifically doesn't work?

MANAGER   Well I've been trying it for a few weeks now, and performance has stayed just the same.

COACH   So what could you do differently?

MANAGER   I could go back to doing what I was doing before.

COACH   Which was what?

MANAGER   Telling people, showing them, motivating them.

COACH   And how was that working?

MANAGER   All right.

COACH   What levels were people performing at?

MANAGER   About the same as now.

COACH   So what are you doing differently?

MANAGER   Coaching them.

COACH   Describe to me specifically what you did on this last session with Sally.

MANAGER   I got her to tell me what she was doing wrong.

COACH   How did you do that?

MANAGER   I got her to explain to me what she could have done better.

COACH   So what were you actually saying to her?

MANAGER   That she could have done something better.

COACH   What in particular did you focus on?

MANAGER   I asked her what there was about the way she opened the presentation that she could have done better.

COACH   What's the difference between telling her that the opening could have been better, and asking what there was about the opening being better?

MANAGER   Well she came up with the answer.

COACH   Alex, what was there about the opening few minutes of your coaching session that could have been handled better, allowing Sally to express herself before you manipulated her into saying that she could have done the opening better?

MANAGER   Just a minute. Are you saying that I didn't coach her properly in the opening few minutes?

COACH   Is that similar to what you did to Sally?

There was a pause. The penny dropped.

COACH   Alex, what was the result of this coaching session on Sally's next call?

MANAGER   It wasn't a great deal better.

COACH   And what have been the results of most of your coaching sessions with others?

MANAGER   I've already told you, not a lot has changed.

COACH   So what could you do differently?

MANAGER   OK so I could try to ask the questions differently.

COACH   What in particular?

MANAGER   Let them express themselves more.

COACH   What effect would that have?

MANAGER   It would commit them to change if they came up with it in the first place.

COACH   How would that make you feel?

MANAGER   I'd be happy if they improved.

COACH   What are you feeling at the moment?

MANAGER   Frustrated.

COACH   What about?

MANAGER   Well, I know what to say. It's just that . . .

COACH   Just what?

MANAGER   Sometimes it just doesn't come out right.

COACH   So what could you do about it?

MANAGER   Practise it more.

COACH   What support do you need?

MANAGER   I'd appreciate it if you continued to give me some feedback.

It took a few more sessions before Alex grasped the fact that he was manipulating responses, not empowering people. Obviously it would be impossible for you to coach all managers, but every now and then you have to step in and help. The ideal metacoach for the manager is the manager's line manager. You can provide that service but it would be better for the manager's manager to do it. That is why you need senior management support. It allows you to play a free role, stepping in and facilitating when appropriate.

Summary

- POWER coaching is a flexible tool which can be easily adapted from performance enhancement to appraisals and goal setting.
- Coaching sessions can be as long or as short as you like, although it is recommended to keep them brief; they can be formal or informal; and can help managers establish better relationships with subordinates through a more participative approach.

9 Epilogue

So where to from here? A major part of the coaching philosophy is the development of personal bests. This must also apply to you as a developer of coaches. I have therefore included in this final chapter, some ideas and suggestions for your own personal development.

Study

I read somewhere that to stop learning is to stop living. I am often asked if I can recommend something to read for people interested in a particular business subject such as training, management, or selling. My feeling is that anything and everything is worth reading. Even if, after reading a complete book, or article, you gauge that there was nothing new, or you did not particularly enjoy it, it is still worth the effort. People spend a great deal more time and energy feeding their bodies than their minds. Some people stretch their bodies to the limit in a vain attempt to stay young or healthy, and yet hardly ever consider how to keep their minds young and healthy. Just because you are trying to be a coach, and many of the analogies we use come from the athletics world, it does not mean that you have also to end up being a prime contender for a gold medal in the marathon. All things in moderation. However, the health of your brain will ultimately give you a great deal more pleasure and reward than the health of your body. I have heard the maxim 'healthy mind, healthy body' and for me it is all a matter of intensity. People have a tendency to gravitate towards a particular area of interest, and at times keeping physically fit and keeping mentally fit seem to be polarized. If I had a choice I'd choose the latter. If you can achieve a balance so much the better, but if time is at a premium, and for most of us it is, then keep your mind alive.

The thing about study is that even if you do not appear to be taking it in, in it goes. The brain has an awesome capacity for recording information. Some communication experts may tell you that items which go into our short-term memory are eventually discarded. Only those that we store in our long-term memory can be recalled. Personally I did not know we had a choice. When things happen to me I do not make a conscious decision to put the experience in my short-term or long-term memory. It just floats around. Sometimes I remember things, sometimes I do not. It is not memory that is the problem, it is recall. If we knew how, we could recall everything that had ever happened to us. Everything we have ever said, done, or seen, is recorded, the problem is we sometimes lose the key. There are those people who develop incredible recall processes, and I do not doubt that given the correct coaching we could all learn how to do it. In the meantime, why take the chance that you might miss something. You, like me, will from time to time have remembered something but not where it came from. It came from a time when you read it, saw it or experienced it. If you fail to keep those experiences going then you run the risk of closing down your ability to develop new ideas and new approaches.

If you can, put your studies on a formal footing. Take a prescribed course of study. If you have already got a degree, take another one. The formality of academic study, at whatever level, can help maintain your impetus for self-improvement.

In terms of the job that we do, then the only recommendation I can make is that you focus on communication. It is communication that shapes the world. I heard a superb quote from Stephen Hawking the other day, 'Man's greatest achievements have come through talking. Man's greatest failures have come about through not talking.' It is fact that the twentieth century, and the increase in communication, has paradoxically reduced our ability to talk to each other. Part of this has to be that information is so readily available in visual form that people have lost the ability to find out things for themselves. Yet the volume of information available in written form is far greater than anything you will see on video or television.

Vision, visualization, self-esteem and self-talk

What is it that draws you to a particular person? There are those people who appear to attract followers, and yet why it happens remains a mystery. They appear to exude a confidence that is difficult to quantify but which has an effect on people they come into contact with. In my studies into leadership and management interventions I came across a phenomenon called 'charismatic leadership'. There are leaders who produce in their followers a sense of mission, of belonging, and a desire for achievement based on the needs for intrinsic reward. These people give reference to the achievements of the past, postulate a vision of the future, and influence action in the present. Charismatic leaders have vision: they seem to have the ability to get us to actually see the success of the future. They are few and far between.

In discussion with people who have achieved success in one form or another, a recurring theme was visualization. People who are successful or who achieve something see it as a natural extension of their planning process. Success rarely comes as a surprise to the successful. They are geared up for it. They saw it some time ago and told themselves it would happen. It is an old conundrum—are people confident because they are successful, or are people successful because they are confident? Where does confidence come from? Some people will say it comes from within. If that is true, then we all have it. Perhaps some just hide it better than others. The Catch 22 of confidence is that it comes from other people, who believe you are confident, because you act confidently. It has to do with the conversations you have with yourself—your self-esteem.

Those people who have a great self-esteem regularly tell themselves that they are on the journey to achieving their goals, and that they will succeed. In developing your coaching relationships with your trainees, you will become a role model for their aspirations, not in terms of their personal goal but of the manner in which they approach it. While motivation is a personal thing, the people you are coaching will be looking to you for inspiration. You can supply it by showing them how to feel confident in their own abilities by showing them how confident you are in your own. The feeling of your own self-worth is the single most important winning quality. It does not simply involve a pride in what you have achieved, or even in what you intend to achieve, but a real joy in accepting who you are right now.

The biggest problem many people face is that they have no vision of the future. Your job is to help people develop that vision by expressing your own. The main reasons why people do not achieve their goals is that most are not written down, and very few are verbally expressed. If you have a goal, write it down; and if you want the people you are coaching to achieve their goal, get them to write theirs down. In the process of writing down a goal it becomes evident that a goal statement alone is worthless. To achieve a goal, you have to know where you are now, where you want to be, and work out how to get there. Most people never write their goals down and as a consequence never begin the journey.

As a coach you should keep and regularly update your own personal development plan. What are you trying to achieve as a coach? What knowledge, skills and behaviours do you need to adopt, and what level are you currently at? It will soon become apparent that you also need a coach. So get one. If you expect to sell the idea of coaching to managers and to trainees then they will look at you for an example. If you demonstrate that you believe that you know it all and do not need a coach, then they will assume the same of themselves.

A useful tool might be to use the format in Appendix 4. Complete your own personal plan before asking others to complete theirs, and if asked, share it with them. You should in any event have a development plan for each of your trainees, and encourage managers to keep a record of achievement of each of their staff.

Lastly, get into the habit of seeing yourself achieve, and help the people you are coaching to see themselves achieving. It involves nothing more simple than closing your eyes and seeing yourself delivering your best performance. Play the scene through in your mind until you can see, hear and feel the performance. If something goes wrong during this scene setting, rewind and put it right, until you see yourself delivering the perfect performance you want. Then repeat it as often as time allows before delivering the performance in reality. It is at this stage that fantasy and reality merge. The scene you have played through in your mind, can and will happen.

A word of warning

Your effect as a coach on the performance of others can be dramatic. You could be the catalyst for immense change, and for feelings of self-worth and achievement not previously experienced by the people you coach. It is at this stage that the relationship you build of support and trust can become a crutch which when you try and remove it results in a collapse of performance and of self-confidence. At all times you must ensure that people understand that their increase in performance has come from them and not from you. You are a facilitator, but you are not the reason for their new found success.

Unless you develop in them a sense of their responsibility for performance increase, and of their ability to sustain and improve that performance, then you could end up having to support them for life, and that just cannot work.

Avoid trying to change people's personal lives. I know that your personal life can have an effect on your work performance, but that is a matter for people to resolve themselves, not for you as a coach to become enmeshed in. If you become involved in helping them to resolve personal issues, you will walk across the boundary between a work coach and a personal counsellor and confidant(e). People may want to see you as such and will attempt to share with you their personal problems, but where you can, avoid it.

Coaching can be a draining experience, and you therefore need to focus on what you can and cannot reasonably achieve. That is not to say that coaching technique cannot help people resolve their personal difficulties, it is just that as an organizational coach I cannot see how you can be all things to all people. The biggest problem you will have, is that in experiencing the power of coaching, in sensing your complicity in the achievement of others, and in the satisfaction of your own personal achievement, you will also be susceptible to believing that in some way all things are possible.

Your job is to give others the confidence to believe in their own ability to solve their own problems without you.

Their confidence will come from the realization that they have the ability to carry out a particular task you give them or that they have previously been unsuccessful at accomplishing. You need to give them a battle they can win, so they will go on to win bigger battles. Start with things they can do, before giving them tasks they believe they cannot achieve.

Their confidence will come from their individual ability to do what is asked of them in their current roles, and this means good quality induction training. Most people fail in new jobs, not because they have not got the ability, but because the induction training was lacking in sufficient direction and initial instruction about what is expected and how to do it. Make sure before you begin coaching someone to increased performance, that he or she has received enough initial training.

People's confidence will come from others around them, from those with whom they work. The job of your managers is to give the team a vision of collective achievement. And lastly, as I have already discussed, confidence comes from the fact that mistakes are tolerated. The best people you have will test the boundaries of your tolerance, and the tolerance of your company.

Conclusion

Is coaching the answer we have all been looking for? I do not know. What I do know is that it is a better way to manage and to develop people than any other form of development I have yet seen or experienced. But if I am also to practise what I preach then I will keep an open mind to the possibility of new developments that can be of use. In the meantime, I am convinced that by adopting the process contained in this book, you too will experience the powerful effect of POWER COACHING.

Appendix 1 **Team ratings**

Team members	Rating of success

Appendix 2 **How you treat people**

My top performers	How I treat them
My bottom performers	How I treat them

Appendix 3 **Observation and feedback**

Metacoach ....   Coach...................

Person being coached...................   Purpose of session..................

Establishing purpose and parameters
Objectives and options
Reasons for current performance
Empowerment of person being coached
Review (if appropriate)
Manager's comments

How to use Appendix 3— Observation and feedback

The purpose of this form is to provide a record of the coaching sessions and also to encourage a dialogue of personal achievement between the coach and the person being coached.

The first two sections are self-explanatory.

The third section (Reasons for current performance) allows the person being coached to verbalize what may well be excuses, or even valid reasons. Whatever the case, by verbalizing the items, it becomes easier to encourage the individual to develop solutions.

The fourth section (Empowerment of the person being coached) is used to ask the person being coached what he or she is going to do about moving performance forward; within what time-scale; and then to instruct him or her to do so.

The fifth section (Review) may not be applicable if no agreement has been reached to move forward, but nevertheless the attempt should be recorded.

The last section (Manager's comments) allows the manager to write down and then to verbalize to the person being coached the benefits the manager has achieved from the session, as well as seeking the thoughts and feelings of the individual.

Appendix 4 **Personal Development Plan**

Things I have to do to move towards my vision	*People who could help me*
My vision of the future	
My experiences of the past	*Things I have already learnt about myself*

Index

Further titles in the McGraw-Hill Training Series

MEETING MANAGEMENT
A Manual of Effective Training Material
Leslie Rae
ISBN 0-07-707782-2

LEARNING THROUGH SIMULATIONS
A Guide to the Design and Use of Simulations in Business
and Education
John Fripp
ISBN 0-07-707588-9 paperback
ISBN 0-07-707789-X Disk

IMAGINATIVE EVENTS Volumes I & II
A Sourcebook of Innovative Simulations, Exercises,
Puzzles and Games
Ken Jones
ISBN 0-07-707679-6 Volume I
ISBN 0-07-707680-X Volume II
ISBN 0-07-707681-8 Set Ringbinder

**TRAINING TO MEET THE TECHNOLOGY
CHALLENGE**
Trevor Bentley
ISBN 0-07-707589-7

CLIENT-CENTRED CONSULTING
A Practical Guide for Internal Advisers and Trainers
Peter Cockman, Bill Evans and Peter Reynolds
ISBN 0-07-707685-0

TOTAL QUALITY TRAINING
The Quality Culture and Quality Trainer
Brian Thomas
ISBN 0-07-707472-6

SALES TRAINING
A Guide to Developing Effective Salespeople
Frank S. Salisbury
ISBN 0-07-707458-0

CAREER DEVELOPMENT AND PLANNING
A Guide for Managers, Trainers and Personnel Staff
Malcolm Peel
ISBN 0-07-707554-4

DESIGNING AND ACHIEVING COMPETENCY
A Competency-Based Approach to Developing People and
Organizations
Edited by Rosemary Boam and Paul Sparrow
ISBN 0-07-707572-2

SELF-DEVELOPMENT
A Facilitator's Guide
Mike Pedler and David Megginson
ISBN 0-07-707460-2

TRANSACTIONAL ANALYSIS
A Handbook for Trainers
Julie Hay
ISBN 0-07-707470-X

USING VIDEO IN TRAINING AND EDUCATION
Ashly Pinnington
ISBN 0-07-707384-3

DEVELOPING WOMEN THROUGH TRAINING
A Practical Handbook
Liz Willis and Jenny Daisley
ISBN 0-07-707566-8

HOW TO SUCCEED IN EMPLOYEE DEVELOPMENT
Moving from Vision to Results
Ed Moorby
ISBN 0-07-707459-9

MAKING MANAGEMENT DEVELOPMENT WORK
Achieving Success in the Nineties
Charles Margerison
ISBN 0-07-707382-7

**HOW TO DESIGN EFFECTIVE TEXT-BASED
OPEN LEARNING**
A Modular Course
Nigel Harrison
ISBN 0-07-707355-X

**HOW TO DESIGN EFFECTIVE COMPUTER-BASED
TRAINING:**
A Modular Course
Nigel Harrison
ISBN 0-07-707354-1

EVALUATING TRAINING EFFECTIVENESS
Translating Theory into Practice
Peter Bramley
ISBN 0-07-707331-2

**MANAGING PERSONAL LEARNING AND
CHANGE**
A Trainer's Guide
Neil Clark
ISBN 0-07-707344-4

DEVELOPING EFFECTIVE TRAINING SKILLS
Tony Pont
ISBN 0-07-707383-5

THE BUSINESS OF TRAINING
Achieving Success in Changing World Markets
Trevor Bentley
ISBN 0-07-707328-2

**PRACTICAL INSTRUCTIONAL DESIGN FOR OPEN
LEARNING MATERIALS**
A Modular Course Covering Open Learning, Computer
Based Training, Multimedia
Nigel Harrison
ISBN 0-07-709055-1

All books are published by:

McGraw-Hill Book Company Europe
Shoppenhangers Road, Maidenhead, Berkshire SL6 2QL, England
Tel: (01628) 23432   Fax: (01628) 770224